NATURE FACTS

FLOWERS

LYS DE BRAY

At first sight, flowers seem to be simply
passive expressions of spontaneous beauty
that brighten our natural environment, but
a closer look reveals that the world of
flowers is every bit as competitive as the
noisiest jungle. In the race to reproduce
their kind, plants have honed their flowers
to a razor edge of specialization to attract
the right kind of pollinating creatures.
Colour, scent, size and shape all figure in
their armoury of beguiling devices. Some
flowers even trap insects until they have
fertilized the tiny eggs that will ensure the
next generation. With such an exciting
story to tell, this book cannot fail to
fascinate all who enquire within.

The opening section of the book provides a
general introduction to the world of
flowers, 'setting the scene' for the more
detailed views that follow. The bulk of the
book takes the form of a series of spread-
by-spread storyboards that focus on
particular flowers and their way of life. In
these spreads, the main text provides the
factual foundation of the story, and the
captions to the photographs carry the
narrative further by focusing on particular
aspects of interest. At the right-hand
margin, a fact file column presents a
miscellany of factual items related to the
main theme of the storyboard. This
approach is echoed in a final 'superfacts'
section that further enhances the reference
value of the book. Throughout, the
emphasis is on presenting the information
in a readable, non-technical and attractive
way that captivates the eye while
feeding the mind.

The orange anthers of *Lilium* Citronella contrast brightly with the pale yellow, recurved, delicately spotted petals.

■ NATURE FACTS ■
FLOWERS

Wild purple violets belong to a family that has spread through
the USA and Europe from its home in the Andes.

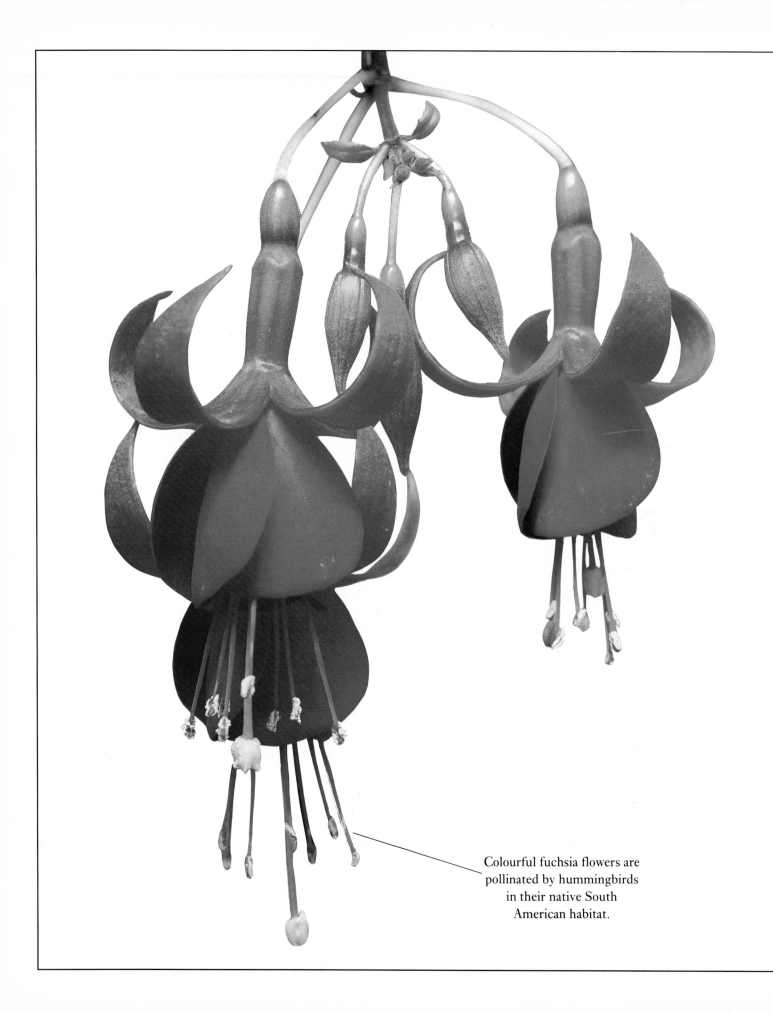

Colourful fuchsia flowers are pollinated by hummingbirds in their native South American habitat.

NATURE FACTS

FLOWERS

LYS DE BRAY

Vanda Thonglor, an orchid raised in Thailand, has rose-coloured petals, strikingly marked with deep crimson.

Grange
BOOKS

Published by Grange Books
An imprint of Grange Books Limited
The Grange
Grange Yard
London
SE1 3AG

Reprinted 1993
CLB 2590
© 1992 CLB Publishing, Godalming, Surrey
Printed and bound in Italy by New Interlitho
All rights reserved
ISBN 1-85627-349-0

The Author
Lys de Bray started to draw wild flowers in 1972 and turned to colour
work two years later. Her botanical drawing and painting won her a Fellowship
of the Linnean Society and Royal Horticultural Society
medals and her work sold throughout the UK, Europe and the USA.
Lys de Bray's flower designs have appeared on silverware, china and
stationery. From painting and drawing, her interest widened to include
writing, and she has published books on wild flowers, the cottage
garden year, shrubs, borders and the green garden.

Credits
Edited and designed: Ideas into Print, Vera Rogers and Stuart Watkinson
Layouts: Jill Coote
Picture Editors: Annette Lerner, John Kaprielian
Photographs: Photo Researchers Inc., New York
Commissioning Editor: Andrew Preston
Production: Ruth Arthur, Sally Connolly, David Proffit, Andrew Whitelaw
Director of Production: Gerald Hughes
Typesetting: Ideas into Print
Colour Separations: Scantrans Pte. Ltd., Singapore

Cultivated for many centuries, roses have been
used for medicinal, religious and commercial
purposes, as well as decoration.

CONTENTS

What is a flower?

Most flowers have a fairly simple structure, although some species, such as orchids, have evolved into amazing shapes. Around the outer edge most flowers have a set of leaflike parts called sepals. When these are green and cup-shaped, they are jointly known as the calyx, which protects the bud from frost and other damage. Within the sepals are the petals, collectively called the corolla. Petals can take many different forms and colours and are designed to attract pollinators. In some flowers, parts of the petals have become modified to form nectaries that produce sugary nectar to tempt and reward pollinating creatures. The sepals and petals together are called the perianth; in certain flowers, such as the tulip and bluebell, they are

This cross-section of a tulip shows the main parts of a typical flower. The 'design' varies in different flowers, but the basic structure remains the same.

These wild cherry flowers have an open accessible shape that makes pollination easy for visiting insects.

Petals
(Designed to attract pollinators to the flower)

Anther   Filament

Stamen (male)

Ovary   Style   Stigma

Carpel (female)

Not all flowers have petals when they open. These bottlebrush flowers are a mass of colour produced by the brilliant red filaments of the stamens. The sepals and petals fall away as the buds open, leaving the stamens to attract pollinators.

very similar. Within the petals are the reproductive parts of the flower. Most flowers contain both male and female parts, although some species have separate male and female flowers on the same plant or even on entirely distinct plants. The female parts occupy the centre of the flower and consist of a carpel, or a number of carpels, each with a swelling at the base called the ovary that contains one or more ovules, each enclosing an egg cell. Once the egg cell is fertilized, each ovule develops into a seed. From the swollen part of the carpel arises a thin structure called the style, on top of which is the stigma which, when ripe, has a receptive surface intended for pollen grains. Some flowers have separate carpels, each with individual styles, or the carpels may be joined together and have one shared style. The ovary may have only one ovule, as in the plum or cherry, or it may have several or even thousands of ovules, as in the orchids. Outside the carpels are the male parts of the flower – the stamens – usually arranged in a circle. Each stamen has a

Hibiscus flowers last for only a day, but their bright colour, ample nectar and effective pollinating structure attract insects and hummingbirds. As the birds sip nectar, pollen is dusted onto their heads and transferred to the next flower on a different plant.

stalk, the filament, topped by a pollen sac, or anther, which is filled with a yellow powder, often finer than dust. Each speck of powder is a pollen grain, containing a male cell that can fertilize the egg cell within the ovule in the female part of a flower. All flowers have stamens and carpels, either separately or together in one flower, but many have evolved along different routes and may have modified the other floral parts, including the sepals, petals and nectaries. Flowers are thus the 'sex organs' of plants, designed to ensure fertilization of the egg cells and the production of a new generation through the agency of seeds. How flowers attract and use pollinating creatures (as well as take advantage of natural forces such as wind and water) is a fascinating story of ingenuity and adaptation – a story we explore in the following pages.

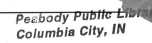
11

The evolution of flowers

Until the dinosaurs disappeared from earth, most of the vegetable kingdom consisted of tree-ferns (cycads), gingkos and conifers. These plants bore their ovules on open scales and have been called gymnosperms from the Greek *gymnos* meaning 'naked', and *sperm*, a 'seed'. Along with mosses, ferns and horsetails, they had developed from primitive algae and seaweeds. At the beginning of the Cretaceous period, about 135 million years ago, a new type of plant began to evolve. In these, the ovules were encased in an ovary and they were named angiosperms from the Greek *angeion*, meaning a 'container'. This was a distinct advance in evolutionary terms, paving the way for the development of a huge variety of flower structures and new methods of pollination and seed dispersal. The gymnosperms had flowers, but they were relatively simple wind-pollinated structures; in the angiosperms, flowers really began to play a part in plant evolution. The angiosperms began to dominate the plant kingdom and evolved rapidly until the end of the Cretaceous period, about 65 million years ago, when there were about 250,000 different species. Most of these had evolved or adapted to be pollinated by insects, with flowers adopting different 'designs' and rewarding their beneficial 'visitors' with nectar and pollen. It is fortunate that the structure of pollen grains is unique to each species of plant and that fossilized pollen can be found in soil deposits millions of years old. By studying tiny pollen grains, scientists have been able to trace the early development of flowering plants.

Many plants began to develop specialized shapes and structures to defend their seed against being eaten by pollinating insects, which also evolved in parallel with the flowering plants. It is thought that in the Cretaceous period, a kind of magnolia evolved from which all the other flowers we know today arose. This early type of magnolia probably

Primitive carpels may have consisted of leaf blades folded around the ovules.

Early stamens may have consisted of flattened leaves with spore-bearing organs on both sides near the tip.

The first flowers might have looked like a magnolia.

Typical of gymnosperms, the pink, female flowers of the larch bear naked ovules. Once fertilized, these become the seeds in the ripe cones.

The female plants of the primitive cycads bear 'naked' seeds on these conelike structures.

Some cycads may be 1,000 years old.

had large quantities of stamens, carpels and petals growing in a spiral shape, and would have been pollinated by cumbersome and clumsy beetles that chewed their way through the stamens. In time, these floral parts decreased, changed and fused into a circle, further evolving to regular radial symmetry. The bilateral shapes of some of today's flowers have developed only very recently, relatively speaking. Flowers have evolved into complex, beautiful and highly practical structures. And they are still evolving today – although magnolias still suffer those blundering beetles!

The emergence of plant life	
QUATERNARY 1.8 million years ago	All plant life flourished. First horses, whales and bats appeared. Emergence of man.
TERTIARY 65 million years ago	Development of mammals.
CRETACEOUS 136 million years ago	Angiosperms emerge and become the dominant flowering plants. End of the dinosaurs. First true birds.
JURASSIC 190 million years ago	First flowering plants. From fossil pollen, it is possible to date species, rocks and climate. Insects took up the role of pollinators.
TRIASSIC 230 million years ago	Ferns and cycads flourished. Conifers moved into deforested tracts left by Permian ice and were the most developed form of plant life, with cones bearing ovules and pollen sacs. First mammals and dinosaurs.
PERMIAN 280 million years ago	Ice age. First cycads emerge.
CARBONIFEROUS 345 million years ago	More primitive plant forms and first conifers, ancestors of redwoods and pines. Vast forests covered the earth. When the trees died, their fallen trunks became petrified into coal. First reptiles.
DEVONIAN 405 million years ago	Seaweeds photosynthesized at greater depths. Mosses and liverworts developed leaves and stems. Giant horsetails, ferns and club mosses grew to 30m(100ft). Seed ferns evolved. First amphibians and insects.
SILURIAN 430 million years ago **ORDOVICIAN** 500 million years ago	Primitive seaweeds, simple club mosses, fungi. One of the first small land plants, *Psilophyton*, developed root hairs.
CAMBRIAN 600 million years ago	Bacteria, algae, blue-green algae. First fish.

Flower shapes

Flowers have taken over 100 million years to evolve from the first primitive shapes into the beautiful and complex structures that we know today. The first simple flowers developed an open, hemispherical shape, followed by an almost flat, radially symmetrical flower. From then on the path of evolution diverged successively to include open, saucerlike flowers with fixed numbers of petals, to more three-dimensional, cone-shaped flowers and finally to the complex shapes of many 'modern' orchids. As we have seen, a flower's main aim is to attract a pollinator and its first inducement is visual impact, namely colour, size and shape. A very large shape has not proved the best; an insect gets lost around the edge, and wastes time and effort wandering about. The social honeybee seems to prefer segmented or uneven outlines and shapes, such as

This wild geranium flower, (*Geranium maculatum*), has a simple open shape with well-defined markings to guide insect pollinators. Note the five-part plan - five petals, ten stamens and five stigmas.

The colour, size and funnel shape make these morning glory flowers very attractive to a range of insect visitors.

Five petal lobes join up to make the bells of the campanula flower, enclosing a three-lobed stigma. Social honeybees are among the insects drawn to these blooms.

This stunning cymbidium is among the most beautiful of the orchids and an excellent example of a highly evolved complex flower. The anther and stigma are borne in the centre, ideally placed for visiting insects to cross-pollinate the flowers.

funnels or bells. Helpful guide markings lead the insect visitor to the centre of the flower, where there is a reward of nectar. Some flowers, like those of the snapdragon family, have further adapted by narrowing or pinching their corollas to protect their sexual organs and nectar. Violets and columbine have developed 'spurs' at the back of the flower that contain nectar, and honeysuckle flowers are long, narrow cornucopias that can be reached only by long-tongued insects.

Orchid flowers are typically long-lasting and constructed on a six-part plan. There are three sepals and three petals - all coloured - the lower petal being modified into a conspicuous lip, or labellum, bearing bright markings to guide pollinating insects into the centre of the flower.

The campanulas have many attractions to offer insect visitors: there are many open flowers on each stem, with several stems to each plant; the flowers are a striking colour and have a protectively deep bell shape; and there is plenty of nectar and pollen.

15

Nature's flower arrangements

As well as producing a variety of flower shapes, the evolution of flowering plants has given rise to a host of natural flower arrangements for us to enjoy and pollinators to exploit. A group of flowers massed together on a single stem is called an inflorescence and flying insect pollinators like them because they can walk from one flower to another without using additional energy in becoming airborne. There are several distinct shapes of inflorescences and all have their advantages. One of the simplest 'floral designs' is the raceme, in which flowers are borne on

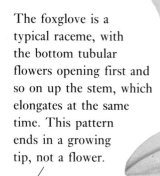

The foxglove is a typical raceme, with the bottom tubular flowers opening first and so on up the stem, which elongates at the same time. This pattern ends in a growing tip, not a flower.

The apparently simple flower of this annual sunflower is in reality a bouquet made up of many smaller florets. This arrangement is known as a capitulum and is a good example of radial symmetry. In the centre there are masses of closely packed, small, deep flowers called disc florets surrounded by a row or rows of flowers each with one large yellow ray-petal, called ray florets.

short stems arranged alternately up the main stem. The bottom flowers open first and new buds form higher up as the main stem elongates. A spike is similar but has many crowded, unbranched flowers, also opening from the bottom upwards, as in lavender. Panicles are loosely branched arrangements that are, in effect, compound racemes and can contain many hundreds of flowers. Where the lower stems in a raceme are much longer than the upper ones, the inflorescence becomes flattened out like a plate to form a corymb, with the short-stemmed flowers in the middle and the long-stemmed ones around the outside. The same kind of shape occurs when all the flower stems are very nearly the same length but radiate out from one point like umbrella spokes. This arrangement is called an umbel. Where each 'spoke' itself ends in an umbel, this is a compound umbel. The ultimate in 'flat' flower arrangements is seen in the capitulum, where small deep flowers are closely packed together at the end of the stem, as in the daisy family.

Comfrey produces a one-sided sequence of tubular flowers that often change colour with age. This arrangement, called a cyme, ends with a flower.

The giant hogweed is a fine example of a compound umbel, with radiating spokes ending in further, smaller radiating wheels of simple flowers. The whole inflorescence forms a firm platform for alighting insects.

Principles of pollination

The main function of flowers is to achieve sexual reproduction by transferring the male cells (pollen) to the female cells (ovules). This is called pollination. When a pollen grain lands on a receptive stigma, a tube grows down through the style to the ovary to reach the ovules. The tube usually enters the ovule through a minute aperture and discharges two nuclei that have travelled down inside the tube from the pollen grain. This journey can take anything from a day to a year. The leading nucleus divides into two, the first fusing with the female egg cell to form the first cell of the embryo plant. The second nucleus fuses with the embryo sac to form nutritive tissue that will feed the developing seed. The pollen grains and egg cells of similar species match as do locks and keys, so that there is no possibility of either accidental or mistaken fusion. One cannot, for example, cross a rose with a

delphinium in order to achieve the much desired truly blue rose. If the pollen from one flower is transported to the stigma of another flower of a similar type, but on a different plant, this is called cross-pollination and is the best method of ensuring a good mixing of genetic material. Self-pollination occurs when pollen is transported to the flower's own stigma or to a different flower on the same plant. Many plants have evolved a balance between the two methods. Insect pollination is the most common and successful method of cross-pollination, because flowers and insects have evolved such close bonds, accounting for about 80 percent of successful fertilization among flowering plants. To prevent accidental self-pollination caused by an insect brushing pollen onto a flower's own stigma, flowers have developed different protective strategies. In willowherb and mallow, for example, the sexual parts

A pencil pushed into the centre of an orchid flower picks up the pollen masses just like an insect would. Notice how they stand erect.

When the pencil is brought close to another flower, the pollen masses point forwards to make contact with the stigma for cross-pollination.

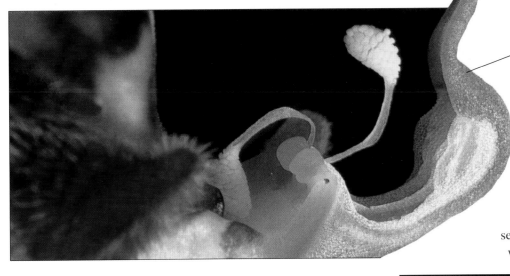

Here one of the pollen masses, or pollinia, of an orchid flower has sprung back against the flower's own stigma, carrying out self-pollination.

The male flowers of a Norway spruce scatter pollen grains into the air. Borne on the wind, the dustlike pollen grains alight onto the stigmas of the separate female flowers on the same plant, which will eventually form into cones.

mature at different times, whereas in holly or hop the male and female flowers occur on different plants. Other plants have an incompatibility system, whereby their stigmas will not accept their own pollen while there is still a possibility of cross-pollination. However, if all else fails and no pollinator appears, the flower accepts its own pollen. The wind accounts for cross-pollination in almost all the remaining 20 percent of flowering plants, occurring in the huge grass family and in many trees and shrubs. It is a most wasteful method, with billions of pollen grains being dispersed. Wind-pollinated flowers are generally recognizable by their subdued coloration, long – often dangling – stamens and large, pollen-trapping, feathery stigmas.

Self-pollination occurs in many plants and is also brought about by insects or the wind or is self-induced. In addition to their normal flowers, violets have evolved to produce extra, non-opening flowers inside which the pollen passes directly from the stamens to the ovary. Some flowers, such as peas and beans are structurally inaccessible to insects. In wheat, barley and oats, the pollen ripens and fertilizes the ovule before the 'flower' opens. The dandelion and the hawkweed have dispensed almost entirely with pollination and their ovules develop into seeds without any form of fertilization.

Markings to guide pollinators

Many members of the viola family, such as this wild pansy, have converging dark lines in the centre of the flowers, which guide insects to the nectar.

Insect visitors to flowers are often helped by ultraviolet 'honey-guide' marks in the form of contrasting spots, dots, lines, patches or encircled areas that stand out clearly and show the insect the way to the food. Geraniums, for example, have converging lines, foxgloves have white-bordered spots that imitate stamens, and toadflaxes have a welcoming yellow or orange patch on the 'lip'. These marks may be invisible to the human eye or, if they are visible to us, they may not be seen as the same colour by a bee. Some markings are ultraviolet against a plain background; other flowers may have a clearly contrasting non-ultraviolet area and, in addition, there may be grooves or channels in the petals to guide the insect's tongue. The wild yellow flag-iris is a good example. This large flower, in the favoured yellow, has three substantial 'landing platforms', called the falls; these are the lower perianth segments - in reality, sepals - with converging black lines that point the way to the nectar. Many flowers, particularly the huge daisy family, have yellow centres and white or coloured petals. This combination is both eye-catching and effective, because yellow is the prime attraction colour. The petals are sterile ray-florets, which also help to attract insects to the yellow disc-florets. Insects are attracted to certain colours that trigger their programmed brains, only visiting flowers with the right colour or combination of colours. In time, some colours change. The horse chestnut, is an excellent example of colour change. When the white flowers open, the centres have smudgy yellow patches that act as signposts to alighting bees seeking nectar. However, when the supply of nectar is exhausted, the yellow patches turn red, which the bees perceive as black, and they cease visiting those flowers.

The flowers of black-eyed Susan, *Rudbeckia hirta*, have ultraviolet-tipped petals. Insects will visit red flowers if they contain ultraviolet. They see green flowers as yellowish and leaves in tones of grey.

The light–bordered dark spots inside a foxglove bell, *Digitalis purpurea*, resemble stamens from a distance and are a clear invitation to bumblebees. The markings are visible to the human eye, as are those in many other flowers. In *Mimulus guttatus*, they are yellow with orange spots; the marsh gentian has rows of light green dots, and the turk's-cap lily has purple spots and a green nectar groove.

21

Flowers pollinated by bats

Not all bats are bloodlusting Transylvanians; many are vegetarian and they relish sweet nectar from flowers. Bat-pollinated flowers share several characteristics. They open at night and are usually white or pale-coloured. Furthermore, the flowers give off either a strong, sweet night-scent or a strong organic odour, that possibly resembles a bat's own smell. Bats are greedy creatures, so the flowers produce large quantities of nectar and pollen, and the flowers and their stems need to be strong enough to support the weight of a clinging bat. Several tropical trees have exceptionally long, strong flowering stems that eventually support huge, heavy fruits. The bat's radar system enables it to land on the flowers without colliding with the trunks or getting entangled in the branches. One such tree, the cannonball tree, has large, sweetly scented, pink-red flowers with two sets of stamens, one surrounding the ovary and the other offset and curving over, rather like a downwardly held hairbrush. Racemes of these very showy flowers hang down around the base of the tree awaiting their bat pollinators, each one supporting as many as a hundred flowers.

Some of the flowers on the cannonball tree grow on the trunk, making them easily accessible to pollinating bats, which cling to the rough bark. Fierce biting ants are visible in the flowers, probably deterring other nectar thieves.

A long-nosed fruit bat approaches a sturdy *Strelitzia* flower, which bears the scars left by other pollinating visitors. These may include other bats, day-flying sunbirds or sugarbirds. They are all attracted to the long crested flowers that resemble the head of a bird, hence this flower's common name, bird of paradise flower.

Glossophaga soricina, the long-tongued bat, is seen here about to alight on the pendulous racemes of *Mabea occidentalis.* It clings to the flowers while feeding on nectar and pollen. About 200 species of bat have adapted to a diet of fruit and nectar.

In their search for sweet nectar, bats fly to and fro along a certain 'beat', returning to the same flower or group of flowers several times in a night and effectively cross-pollinating them.

FACT FILE

❏ Bat claws have been found on the evil-smelling flowers of *Cobaea* plants in Mexico.

❏ The large, white scented flowers of the baobab (above) with their 'dusting-puffs' of stamens, are very attractive to bat pollinators, such as this *Epomorphorus wahlbergi.*

❏ The white, yellow-centred flowers of the giant saguaro cactus are pollinated by insects and desert doves by day, but by hawkmoths and bats during the night.

❏ Bat visitors to the large, yellowish white, bell-shaped flowers of the calabash tree can get a secure grip on its gnarled, spiny bark.

❏ The sausage tree of tropical Africa and Madagascar has long, strong-stemmed flowers suspended far below the leaf canopy. Bats alight on the handsome, crimson, hibiscus-like flowers that give off an unpleasant odour of fermentation. The pollinated flowers give way to 1m(39in)-long sausage-shaped fruits that may touch the ground.

Flowers pollinated by birds

Bird-pollinated flowers are almost always brightly coloured - red, carmine and orange being the favoured shades. Flowers such as fuchsias and prickly pear that are pollinated by hovering hummingbirds usually project sideways or hang down, as the birds need no landing platform. On a typical day, a rufous hummingbird will visit about 1,500 flowers. Sunbird-pollinated flowers are usually strongly constructed and may have convenient, woody perching stems, although birds alighting on the giant *Lobelia deckenii* may damage the rigid tips of the bracts. Bird-pollinated flowers produce abundant nectar, often in long curving tubes to suit the birds' beaks. There are no honey or nectar guides because birds have sharp eyes, but sometimes the corolla tube is a different colour. There is little scent, as a bird's sense of smell is not well developed. Many nectar-drinking birds eat insects as part of their diet and may originally have discovered flower nectar by pleasurable accident. *Spathodea*, the African tulip tree, has brilliant gold-edged, scarlet, cup-shaped blossoms that attract pollinating sunbirds, which perch on the stout, upwardly pointing fruits (made larger by water absorption). *Strelitzia*, the bird of paradise flower, is pollinated by both sunbirds and sugarbirds, which alight on the fused petals. Their landing acts as a lever, forcing the anthers upwards and out of their sheaths, so that they deposit pollen on the bird's breast. The anthers mature before the stigma, which eventually protrudes from the sheath, thus ensuring cross-pollination.

Heliconias have dramatic stems of upright or pendent bracts, all arranged in one plane. Their bright colours attract hummingbirds to the often inconspicuous true flowers nestling within.

The cactus finch buries its beak in a yellow opuntia flower and in the process its head becomes covered with pollen, which will be transferred to the next flower it visits.

As this ruby-throated hummingbird takes nectar from the flower, it unwittingly picks up pollen from the stamen and carries it to another flower.

Thousands of tropical hibiscus blooms provide sweet sugary nectar for hummingbirds in America. Some flowers are pendent, while others are stiffly erect or held at an angle.

❏ There are about 200 different kinds of aloe in Africa and all of them are pollinated by sunbirds, which perch on the sturdy branching flower stems to reach right down into the tubular blooms to get at the nectar and, sometimes, insects. The birds are automatically dusted with pollen as they brush against the stamens.

❏ *Antholyza ringens* from South Africa has evolved a made-to-measure perch for its sunbird and honeybird visitors. Their breasts become well dusted with pollen as they probe deep into the orange-red flowers.

❏ *Holmskioldia*, the Chinese hat plant, originally from the Himalayas, has very bright red flowers that project at exactly the right angle to attract hummingbirds in the semi-tropical gardens of America.

❏ Some South American puyas have thickly crowded lower flower stalks topped with bare stems on which birds perch as they seek the abundant nectar in the flowers.

❏ *Columnea fendleri* from Mexico, and Central and South America has tubular red flowers that produce copious nectar. Hummingbirds visit them regularly, as they do the orange trumpets of *Campsis radicans*, a vigorous climber from the southern United States, which develops aerial roots to help it cling to trees.

Bumbles, beetles and other pollinators

Lured by an abundance of food and nectar, there are a number of regular, opportunistic or accidental pollinators of flowers. Bumblebees are much heavier and stronger than honeybees, and their hairy bodies collect pollen as they go from flower to flower. They also have tough, probing tongues and can obtain nectar from deep-throated flowers, such as *Polyanthus*. The trailing arbutus, *Epigaea repens*, of eastern North America has copious nectar and is sought by queen bumbles busy nest-building . The lady's slipper orchid of northern temperate regions is also visited by queen bumblebees, which are strong enough to push their way into the inflated lower petal of the flower, land on the stigmas and then brush past the paired anthers on their way towards the nectar and the daylight they can discern at the back of the flower. The flowers of the California allspice, with their heady 'wine' scent, open as females and attract beetles. The petals form a dome, effectively imprisoning the beetles that are busily eating a granular food provided by the flower. After a day or so, the flower changes to a male state, the stigmas wither and the anthers open and powder the beetles with pollen. Then the petals open and the beetles are freed, promptly going off to another flower to begin the process all over again. To avoid self-pollination, the flower produces stamenlike growths that protect any stigmas that have not withered.

Flies visit flowers often but irregularly. Their importance in pollination is, therefore, limited, as they have little or no tendency to restrict themselves to one type of flower at a time, as bees do.

The honeybee taking nectar. Sometimes its mouthparts are the wrong size and the flowers will need shorter- or longer-tongued visitors to be pollinated effectively.

Bumblebees have longer tongues than honeybees and very furry bodies to which the sticky pollen adheres.

Some bumbles have pollen baskets on their legs, while others have them on the undersides of their bodies.

The beetle *Malachius bipustulatus* often visits buttercups. It is a real little pollen-sweeping machine, but does little to assist in the process of cross-pollination.

Bees collect pollen moistened with nectar and transfer it to 'pollen baskets' on their hind legs. The pollen is prevented from falling out by specially adapted bristles.

❏ A pale yellow orchid from South America, *Stanhopea graveolens*, generates an extremely unpleasant smell to attract flies when it is ready for pollination. As they visit the flower they are captured by a species of spider lying in wait for them. The spider is in turn greedily consumed by the hummingbird, *Glaucis hirsuta*, which pollinates the flowers at the same time, thus finishing the job that the flies began.

❏ Vertebrate visitors may be occasional but effective pollinators. The little honey mouse from Western Australia, for example, is equipped with a long snout and a longer tongue with which it searches for nectar in tubular flowers. In satisfying its sweet tooth, it fertilizes the flowers, as does a rat in Hawaii that climbs the stems of *Freycinetia arborea* to eat the bracts.

❏ Slugs and snails pollinate *Rhodea japonica*, but damage the fleshy white outer petals in the process.

❏ The chocolate or cocoa tree, *Theobroma cacao,* from tropical America has clusters of surprisingly small and dainty but malodorous pinkish white flowers that spring from the old wood of the tree. The flowers are visited and pollinated by dung-flies attracted by the smell. They also pollinate the Panama tree, *Sterculia apetala*, which has flowers without petals that also smell of freshly dropped dung.

Pollinating partners

Some plant relationships are highly specialized - consider the amazing partnership of the yucca and the yucca moth in the southwestern USA. The yucca cannot pollinate itself because of the position of its anthers and stigma. Its cream, bell-shaped flowers open further at night when it is cooler, and at this time it is visited by several moths, but its main association is with the yucca moth. The female moth has developed specialized mouthparts that enable her to collect the yucca's sticky pollen, which she forms into a ball and carries tucked under her 'chin'. Having gathered enough pollen, the moth flies to another flower on a different yucca plant. It pierces the walls of the ovary with its long ovipositor, lays its eggs, then climbs up to the stigma and spreads the pollen on it, thus ensuring pollination. The eggs hatch and the larvae feed on some of the swelling ovules, which develop in sufficient numbers to ensure the continuation of both moth and plant. The yucca moth eats nothing in its adult state, being only concerned with egg-laying. When it has collected the pollen, spread it on the stigma and laid its eggs, it dies. The larvae hatch out into moths in the following year, just before the yucca is ready to flower. By the time the flowers open, the male moths will have fertilized the females and the cycle can begin again.

A yucca flower with one of its petals cut away to reveal a female yucca moth near the top of the style. The moth 'injects' her eggs into the ovary and in crawling upwards deposits previously collected pollen onto the stigma to fertilize the flower.

The comet orchid flower may have to wait many weeks for a pollinator, so the petals are long lasting and protected from drying out by a waxy covering. The moth is nocturnal, so the flowers are a luminous white.

❑ Fig flowers are born *inside* the fruit, enclosed by the skin, but there is a small hole at one end through which a minute wasp crawls to pollinate the flowers. These can be clearly seen in the cross-section shown above. The female wasp lays its eggs in the ovaries of the fig, and the grubs hatch and develop into adult wasps. These crawl out of the fig, passing over the male flowers and becoming well dusted with pollen as they leave. Then the young female wasps seek out other figs (below) in which to lay their eggs and pollinate the flowers. This relationship, known as caprification, is also seen in the smyrna fig and fig wasp.

Comet orchid flowers have an exceptionally long spur with nectar in the tip. Charles Darwin examined the flower and surmised that there ought to be an insect with a 30cm(12in)-long tongue, able to reach the nectar and pollinate the flower. At that time, no such insect was known and his theory was ridiculed. But about 40 years later, a moth was discovered with a tongue long enough to reach the nectar in the tip of the spur. It was named *Xanthopan morgani praedicta*, the last word commemorating Darwin's prediction of its existence.

The yucca moth, *Tegeticula yuccasella*, is the exclusive pollinator of the yucca. Here, the larvae have started to emerge from the fruit after hatching inside, where they will have fed on some of the seeds.

Single-sex flowers

Nearly all flowering plants are hermaphrodite, which means that they have the male and female parts in one flower. Such flowers have evolved many different methods of avoiding self-pollination, which would cause weakness and general deterioration of the stock within a few generations, and ultimately undermine the strength of the species itself. Single-sex flowers are either male or female. If the separate sexes occur on different plants, they are said to be dioecious, from the Greek 'having two homes'. The primrose, *Primula vulgaris*, is a notable example of a dioecious plant. In the female 'pin-eyed' flowers, the stigma is clearly visible, exactly like a green pinhead in the corolla tube. The male 'thrum-eyed' flowers, on the other hand, have clearly visible stamens. In the wild, natural populations of equal numbers exist, ensuring cross-pollination that results in healthy and vigorous young plants. Bees, butterflies, flies and moths all visit these flowers. Some plants have flowers of different sexes on the same plant, and these are known as monoecious, from the Greek 'single home'. A good example is the hazel, which has long dangling male catkins that toss about in the wind, scattering pollen grains onto the nearby female flowers. These are tiny and budlike, with red styles that resemble small sea anemones. Their wispy threads have sticky surfaces that trap the wind-blown pollen grains.

'Pin-eyed' female primrose flowers. The brimstone butterfly is the principal pollinator of primroses in Europe, putting its long tongue into the base of the pin-eyed form and depositing pollen onto the stigma.

These are 'thrum-eyed' male primrose flowers, with obvious stamens. Visiting butterflies probe deep into the flower and pick up pollen halfway down the proboscis. This is then transferred to the stigmas of the separate female flowers.

Like the hazel, the wind-pollinated Italian alder, *Alnus cordata*, has long, dangling male catkins that shed pollen onto the receptive female catkins. These are usually found close by on the same branch. Here, a shower of yellow pollen granules cascades down from the male flowers onto the red styles of the female flowers below.

❏ Flowers can be single sexed on a time basis instead of by structure. For example, *Persea americana*, a form of avocado that grows wild from Mexico to the Colombian Andes, has two kinds of tree, with flowers of different sexes that open twice, first as females and then as males. One tree will have flowers that open as males in the morning and then close briefly to open again as females in the afternoon. The flowers on the other tree open as females in the morning, close and re-open as males.

❏ The holly is dioecious, only producing berries if bees visit both flower sexes, which occur on separate trees. The berries appear only on the female tree (shown top, male below) Small flowers appear in spring. In poor weather, bees will not venture out to pollinate them.

Flowers without petals

The petal-less (or apetalous) flowers, such as the cornuses, poinsettia and other euphorbias, attract pollinators by means of brilliant scarlet, white or yellow bracts which, to an insect, a bird and most humans, look exactly like petals. The exotic and unreal-looking *Anthurium* has a flat, heart-shaped, puckered red spathe, so shiny that it looks lacquered. In the centre of the flower is a cylindrical cream spadix, packed with flowers, often golden with pollen and very attractive to insects. The *Bougainvillea,* or 'paper flower', throws a wonderful cloak of long-lasting colour over walls, buildings, pillars and trees in tropical countries and along Mediterranean shores. In fact, the three papery 'petals' are really bracts that enclose the small and inconspicuous cream-coloured true flowers. Another apetalous flower is the strangely shaped and coloured Dutchman's pipe (*Aristolochia* spp.), with its flat-faced 'flowers' surrounding the siphon-shaped tube. Some Dutchman's pipes come from temperate regions but most are tropical. Many are strong, twining climbers. The flowers all have a similar basic shape, but some have additional tails or an extended lip, or both. The large-flowered *Clematis* varieties are climbing plants with 'flowers' of all colours except scarlet and bright yellow. But, once again, the 'petals' are actually coloured bracts that attract insect pollinators, although the progeny of these hybrids will not come true and must be propagated vegetatively. The 'pussy willow' has no petals but catkins shaped like rabbit-tails that give off clouds of golden pollen when the wind blows. Later on, the riper pussy willows attract scores of early butterflies and other insects.

The spectacular and abundant blossom of *Eucalyptus ficifolia* is nectar-rich. It produces vast numbers of flowering shoots to compensate for the damage caused by bat pollinators. The tufts of stamens left behind as the sepals and petals drop from the bud are long and colourful.

The dazzling scarlet 'flowers' of the poinsettia are very attractive to hummingbirds, which can see the colour red. The inconspicuous, nectar-rich flowers nestle in the centre of the bright red asymmetrical bracts.

The bougainvillea found in tropical and subtropical countries is famous for the beautiful magenta-purple, papery bracts that surround the small, real flowers in the centre of the plant. There are several types and bract colours, including crimson, pink, salmon, rust and white, which bloom at different times of the year.

Not all the exotic *Anthuriums* are as brightly coloured as these. Some have spathes in quiet shades of green or greenish grey.

Bees and flies are attracted to the abundant pollen in the closely packed flowers on the cylindrical spadix, clearly visible here.

❏ The poinsettia (*Euphorbia pulcherrima*), is grown as a house plant, although in nature it is a large deciduous shrub from Mexico and Central America, which can grow to 3m(10ft).The bright red petals are really bracts that attract pollinators to the tiny flower clusters nearby, with their copious nectar. Pink and white forms of poinsettia are also very beautiful. *Euphorbia fulgens* has tiny yellow flowers surrounded by scarlet bracts and *E. milii*, the crown of thorns, has prickly stems.

❏ There are many species and varieties of *Anthurium*, or painter's palette, with rose, pink, white, crimson and yellow spathes. The spathes provide a highly colourful background for the slender spadix with its cluster of small flowers. These plants come from Colombia and need warm greenhouse conditions elsewhere in the world. Cut flowers last for many weeks.

❏ The *Cornus*, or dogwood, family is large and varied and mostly found in North America, but there are several species from China and Japan. Some are grown for their foliage or bark and some have the large petal-like bracts in shades of pink and white.

❏ Many trees, including willows, alder, hornbeam, oaks, birch and beech, have separate male and female catkins, all of which are pollinated by the wind.

Flowers on a grand scale

Some flowers can attain quite remarkable sizes. One beautiful example is the giant-flowered chalice vine, or cup-of-gold (*Solandra guttata*), from Mexico and the West Indies, with its banana-yellow, trumpet-shaped blooms. They can measure up to 23cm(9in) across. The flowers smell deliciously of coconut and apricots. The yellow lotus lily is the largest-flowered plant in the USA, with leaves standing 1.8m(6ft) out of the water, often overtopped by the huge flowers. The beautiful king protea has enormous flowers made up of outer plum-red bracts downy with silvery hairs, as are the true flowers within. Another protea, *P. barbigera*, produces flowers up to 18cm(7in) across.

Puya raimondii from Bolivia has the largest and tallest inflorescence in the world. It is pictured here next to a man measuring 1.93m(6ft 4in). There can be as many as 8,000 blooms on the spectacular 10.7m(35ft) flower spike.

The enormous flowers of the giant or king protea, *Protea cynaroides*, from South Africa, may measure 28cm(11in) across. The outer plum-red 'petals' are actually bracts. The flowers are sometimes cut for long-lasting flower arrangements, but being slow-growing, many species are protected by law. The plant is named after the Greek sea god Proteus.

The spectacular chalice vine can climb to a height of 9m(30ft). Its scented golden flowers change colour with age. They open so rapidly that their movement can be seen with the naked eye.

FACT FILE

❑ *Cardiocrinum giganteum* is the giant lily from the Himalayas and Tibet that can grow to more than 3m(10ft). It has majestic, creamy white, scented flowers, each one measuring 15-30cm(6-12in).

❑ *Dillenia indica* is a 12.4m(40ft) tree that grows in India, Thailand and Malaya. It produces enormous white flowers measuring about 20cm(8in) across.

❑ A variety of *Aristolochia, A. sturtevantii,* from the West Indies, Central and South America, has gigantic blooms 50cm(20in) long with a 90cm(36in) 'tail' (above). The pelican flower, or swan flower, as it is also known, is the most commonly grown.

The world's largest single flowers

The largest single flower in the world is the rare *Rafflesia arnoldi* from the jungles of Southeast Asia. Its flowers can measure 90cm(36in) across and weigh 6.75kg(15lb). The heavy flowers of this parasitic plant rest on the ground, where they are pollinated by beetles and flies. The plant has no chlorophyll and the huge, fleshy, funguslike petals are red-brown, mottled with white. Little is known about *Rafflesia* because of the difficulties of travelling through the dense tropical rainforest in which it lives, and it has not been possible to reproduce its habitat with sufficient exactness so that it can be grown 'in captivity'. Another enormous flower is the *Amorphophallus titanum* from Sumatra, a giant arum with a crimson spathe up to 2.5m(8ft) high. Like many of the arums, it advertises its readiness for pollination by generating an appalling stench, described as an amalgam of decaying fish and burning sugar, quite delicious to carrion flies. The inflorescence grows at a rate of 7.5cm(3in) a day until fully expanded, but once formed, the flowers only last about six hours.

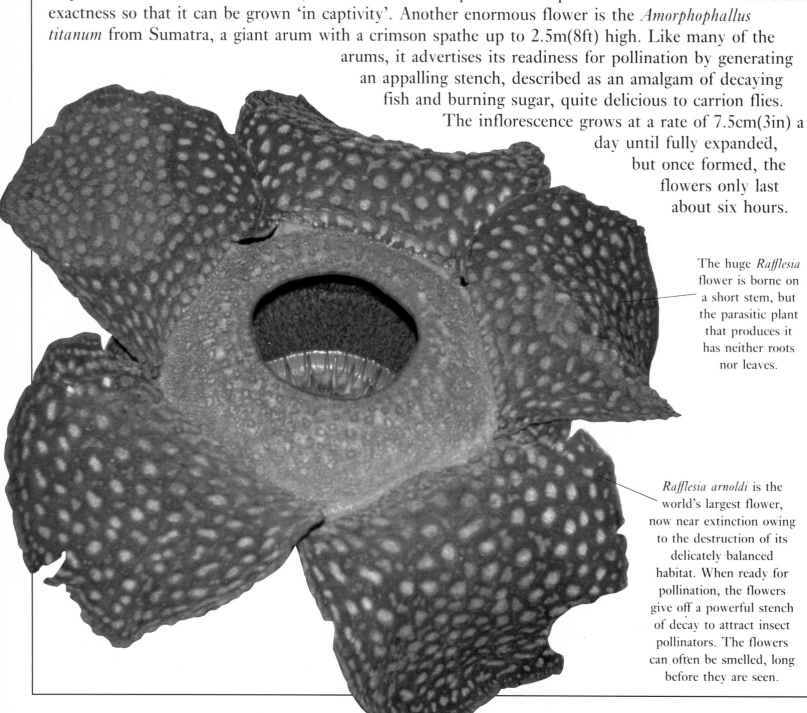

The huge *Rafflesia* flower is borne on a short stem, but the parasitic plant that produces it has neither roots nor leaves.

Rafflesia arnoldi is the world's largest flower, now near extinction owing to the destruction of its delicately balanced habitat. When ready for pollination, the flowers give off a powerful stench of decay to attract insect pollinators. The flowers can often be smelled, long before they are seen.

The striking and unreal-looking flowers of the torch ginger can be as much as 25cm(10in) across on stems over 4m(13ft) tall. The waxy 'petals' surrounding the central cone of flowers are bracts. Shiny and bright colours are attractive to pollinators.

Sustained by tropical warmth, the blooms of *Amorphophallus* eventually reach a large size, but collapse in a matter of hours once they have been pollinated.

In the centre of this large *Amorphophallus* inflorescence the spadix is smothered in male flowers just beneath the cap and the female flowers are located further down.

❏ The extraordinary spathe of *Amorphophallus* (above) can measure up to 2.5m(8.2ft) long with a diameter of 1.2m(4ft). The spadix measures about 107cm(42in) tall, with a diameter of 15cm(6in). When fully grown, the tip may be 4.5m(15ft) from the ground.

❏ The spectacular torch ginger from Indonesia has glossy pink or red 'torches' made up of waxy petal-like bracts. The inflorescence looks its best before the yellow true flowers appear. The flowering stems are formed well away from the canelike leaves.

❏ *Magnolia grandiflora*, as its name suggests, produces large, creamy, lemon-scented blooms, measuring up to 20cm (8in) across, with large shining evergreen leaves.

❏ The largest orchid flower is *Cypripedium caudatum*, with flowers up to 90cm(36in) wide.

The smallest flowers

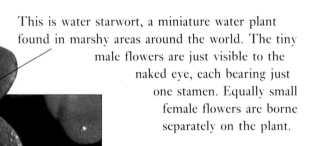

The smallest flowers are those of free-floating duckweeds - simple plants that cover the surface of still ponds and lakes with an apple-green film that is often detrimental to other water plants. Water meal, *Wolffia arrhiza*, is a kind of duckweed that reproduces itself vegetatively, although it also has near-invisible male flowers. These appear from the upper surface of the frond, which is just 0.14mm(0.035in) long. The European greater and lesser duckweeds have marginally larger flowers and dangling roots. An attractive little cushion-shaped plant, the mossy cyphel, has more discernible white flowers that are pollinated by flies collecting nectar. Other plants in the same family have smaller flowers, often with no petals. Another miniature-flowered plant is the cover-all, helxine or 'mind-your-own-business', which has near-invisible separate male and female pink flowers. In Victorian times it was grown as neat-leaved ground cover in vast, humid conservatories, from which it escaped to colonize lawns and larger areas. *Tillandsia usneoides,* or Spanish moss, is a plant of the tropics, found from the southeastern USA through Central and South America. It is an essential part of the Florida landscape, hanging from swamp trees and telephone wires in smoky festoons. The shoots have minute bluish or greenish flowers and are covered with absorbent scales that become filled with air. Birds collect *Tillandsia* as nesting material and man uses it for packaging, so the plant and its seeds are widely scattered.

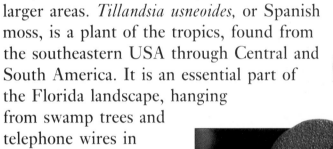

This is water starwort, a miniature water plant found in marshy areas around the world. The tiny male flowers are just visible to the naked eye, each bearing just one stamen. Equally small female flowers are borne separately on the plant.

The tiny white flowers of the mossy cyphel, *Cherleria sedioides*, measure 4-5mm (0.16-0.2in) and sit on top of firm cushions of foliage.

The minuscule flowers of the epiphytic Spanish moss, *Tillandsia usneoides*, appear here among new growth. The plant is a rootless bromeliad living on nutrients in the air.

Mentha requienii from Corsica has peppermint-scented, spreading green mats of minute-leaved foliage which are dotted with the smallest of lilac-mauve flowers.

FACT FILE

❏ A small European land plant, the chaffweed, or bastard pimpernel, has pinkish flowers measuring less than 1mm(0.04in) in diameter.

❏ The water forget-me-not, *Myosotis palustris*, is another aquatic plant with tiny flowers - the blue, yellow-centred blooms measure just 6mm(0.25in) across. The belief that these flowers kept alive sweet memories can be traced back to the fifteenth century. One legend has it that 'forget-me-not' were the last words of a gallant knight who drowned in a stream while trying to collect a bunch of the flowers for his mistress.

❏ *Sinningia pusilla* is a tiny 'Gloxinia' with diminutive yellow-throated mauve flowers that could grow in a thimble.

❏ *Actinotus bellidioides* is a tiny member of the umbellifer family from Tasmania, with minute leaf rosettes only about 2.5cm(1in) tall and even more minute umbels of flowers about 6mm(0.25in) across.

❏ The smallest orchid plant is thought to be *Notylia norae* from Venezuela, while the smallest individual orchid flower is that of *Bulbophyllum minutissimum* from Australia. The Mediterranean smoke tree, *Cotinus coggygria,* has large cloudy inflorescences of the tiniest flowers and *Gypsophila paniculata*, or baby's breath, has thousands of minute white flowers.

Flowers of the night

As daylight fades, many flowers in the temperate regions of the world begin to droop or close their petals for protection against cold or moisture. However, there are flowers that open as the light dims. One of these, the evening primrose, begins to unfold its pale yellow petals in late afternoon and closes them again at dawn. Many night-blooming flowers are white or pale-coloured and often strongly scented to attract pollinating moths. The flowers of the tobacco plant, *Nicotiana*, give off a heavy fragrance when they open in the evening. The night-blooming cereus, or 'queen of the night', is a climbing or trailing cactus that tends to look rather limp and undistinguished by day, but as dusk approaches, its huge flowers begin to open in a great burst of petals, unexpectedly beautiful on the spiny, angled green stems. The moonflower, or moonvine, is related to the morning glories, but unlike them it begins to open its salver-shaped flowers at dusk. These stay open all night and then, as the sun rises, the flowers close, just as the morning glories are beginning to unfold.

In Venezuela, several types of *Cobaea* are fertilized very effectively by nectar-seeking hawkmoths, whose wings pick up pollen that is only released at night. The pollen is transported to other flowers whose stigmas are only receptive after sunset. If the flower has been pollinated, it will start to wither next day.

The true evening primrose has a profusion of tightly folded pale yellow flowers, which gradually begin to open during the afternoon. By early evening, the movement is much faster and the petals can be seen moving as they open in the gathering gloom to entice their moth pollinators, attracted by the pale colour and sweet scent. By morning, when the flowers have been pollinated, they have started to wither.

Daturas hang limp and almost scentless during the day and are pollinated by humming-birds, but at dusk the flowers emit a heady perfume to attract night-flying pollinators and the flowers become firm and shapely.

The night-blooming *Cereus* from Jamaica climbs over rocks or up into trees. Its large, vanilla-scented flowers are yellow and white and may measure 20cm(8in) wide by about 30cm(12in) long.

❏ The marvel of Peru, or 'four o'clock plant', *Mirabilis jalapa*, grows about 60cm(24in) high. It has slightly scented clusters of red, pink, yellow, white or striped flowers (above). The name 'four o'clock plant' is not particularly accurate, as it wakes up any time after lunch, but is wide open and awake by six o'clock in the evening.

❏ The aptly named moonflower *Ipomoea alba*, is a vine from tropical America, growing to 3m(10ft) or more. It is cultivated for its large, fragrant nocturnal flowers, which grow to about 15cm(6in) wide.

❏ In India, the tree of sadness (night jasmine) has very fragrant but shortlived orange flowers that open at dusk, but have fallen to the ground by dawn. They are sometimes gathered to make perfume.

❏ *Hibiscus trionum*, known as 'flower-of-an-hour'. Its white, cream or yellow flowers, up to 7.5cm(3in) across, open for a few hours in the morning.

❏ The heavy perfume of night-scented stock is released when the flowers open after dark.

Flowers of the sun

When clouds obscure the sun, many flowers can be counted on to close up instantly to protect their delicate generative organs from the drop in temperature and the damage from rain. Others, such as the goat's beard, or 'Jack-go-to-bed-at-noon', open and close at regular times, except in overcast weather. The scarlet pimpernel, or poor man's weather glass, is often the quickest to react to a change in light and temperature, closing firmly until sunlight returns, which may not be until the following day or even week, in some northern regions. The pink flowers of *Oxalis rosea* close equally quickly and the shamrock-leaves form 'tents' if the temperature drops. The plant was a favourite choice in old cottage gardens, set out by doorways as an effective barometer during the plant's long flowering season. Blue-eyed grass, *Sisyrinchium angustifolium*, is particularly sensitive to temperature and light, shutting rapidly when the sun goes in and often not re-opening that day. Without its blue-mauve flowers, the plant is so inconspicuous as to be invisible.
The dazzling Livingstone daisies, *Dorotheanthus bellidiformis*, are glitteringly shiny daisy flowers in many colours, which appear so apprehensive of climatic change that they never open unless the sun is shining directly on the plants; the petals close long before evening. This behaviour is common to other South African flowers, such as the orange *Gazanias*.

In full sun, the light-reflecting petals of these wide-open Livingstone daisies are seen in all their glory. However, when the sun goes in, they close so rapidly that they can be seen to move.

The daisylike flowers of the sun-loving star of the veldt marigold, *Dimorphotheca aurantiaca*, close very quickly when the sky becomes overcast.

Not many insects fly during wet weather, so if adverse conditions persist for long, flowers will not be pollinated.

The flowers of blue-eyed grass wink quickly shut when clouds cover the sun or the temperature changes. These are cautious flowers and when the weather is very changeable they often do not open at all. Closed flower buds are almost invisible.

This photograph of a group of closed Livingstone daisies was taken at 6.30pm on a cloudy evening. If cloud and rain persist for several days, they will not open at all.

FACT FILE

❏ Dandelions and lawn daisies, *Bellis perennis*, close up their flowers when the weather is cool and damp.

❏ Many plants have a fixed flowering season and if they are not pollinated during that time because of adverse weather conditions or a dearth of pollinating insects, they cannot produce viable seed. The lesser celandine (above) a member of the familiar buttercup family, with its myriad yellow stars, gilds sunny banks in early spring and is a prime source of food for bees, flies and early hatching butterflies. However, it closes quickly when the weather deteriorates and does not depend on insect pollinators for the survival of its species. It also produces quantities of bulbils, a form of small skinless bulb, which are carried away from the parent plant by spring rains or moved by other agents, such as animals or gardeners. The bulbils are exceedingly viable, each one guaranteed to produce a healthy little plant for the following year.

A few hours in bloom

Some plants produce a profusion of flowers, each of which may last for only a day or even less. The morning glory's blue moons, for example, open in the summer dawn and close at midday. The day lilies (*Hemerocallis*), live up to their name; each of the several trumpet-shaped scented flowers on the stem lasts for a day, but there are many stems in a well-grown clump. The day flower (*Commelina communis*), is unusual in being one of very few blue flowers. One bud opens each day, but with many buds on each stem, flowers bloom successively. Some of this plant's relatives have such thin-petalled flowers that in hot weather they last just a few hours and then dissolve. The exotic three-petalled *Tigridias* from Mexico have a short but beautiful life; as each flower dies in the evening, another is ready for the following day. The flower-of-an-hour gives much better value than its name would suggest, as in temperate regions the creamy-yellow flowers last all day. The 'blue mahoe' hibiscus flowers from Jamaica last only a day, whether on the bush or when cut, but as they need no water once picked, they are invaluable for ornament and decoration, although they are not used for garlands because they bruise too easily. Hedge and field bindweeds open their funnel-shaped flowers before dawn, but by afternoon they have rolled up their flowers like parasols. The flowers of field bindweed are white or light pink, while the larger hedge bindweed is a deeper shade of pink. The plant is well named, twisting a tight stranglehold around its host plant, often suffocating it. It can be very difficult to eradicate, once it has become firmly established.

In cooler parts of the world the creamy blossoms of *Hibiscus trionum*, aptly named the flower-of-an-hour, last all day, but in tropical areas the flowers fade much faster. Each plant will produce these attractive flowers from midsummer until autumn. Note the dark nectar guides that signal pollinating insects.

Many flowers change colour after fertilization. This blue morning glory will turn pinkish in the afternoon, a signal to pollinators that the flower is fertilized and no longer producing nectar.

The Californian poppy produces a mass of bright orange, four-petalled papery blooms. They push off their protective 'nightcaps' early in the day, but by evening the petals have fallen.

The lovely day lily, *Hemerocallis fulva*, lives up to its name; by early evening, each day's bloom is fading as the next flower prepares to open.

❑ The blue dawn flower (*Ipomoea learii*), is a close relative of the morning glory. It is exceedingly vigorous in warm countries, often growing to 9m(30ft) or more, but cannot withstand frosts.

❑ *Cistus*, pictured above, and commonly known as the rock or sun rose, (although not related to the rose family), is Mediterranean in origin. The plant blooms obsessively for two or three months on end, each crumpled flower lasting less than a day before its petals join all the others on the ground. Many sun roses have well-marked honey-guides.

❑ *Dillenia*, or the Burma simpoh, is a 28m(90ft) forest tree found in Burma, Thailand, Malaya, Indochina and Indonesia. It has 15cm(6in)-wide fluttering golden flowers that appear on the gaunt branches before the leaves are fully expanded. They last just one day, to be followed later by orange fruits.

Sweet scents during the day

Scent is a primitive stimulus, a mixture of many different chemical compounds, some of which carry further than others. Flowers produce their enticing, alluring scents to attract pollinators, and insects use a flower's scent as a direction-finder, flying along the odour trail until they can see the flower. Although scent is principally a guide and signal, recent observations have shown that it also acts as an additional sexual stimulus to male bees and perhaps other insects. Day-scented flowers give off their perfume to attract main pollinators, such as bees of all kinds, butterflies, day-flying moths and other insects. Since there are more day-flying insects and they are also attracted by colour, markings and shape, most flowers get pollinated during the day. The flower rewards its visitors with nectar and/or pollen, and as the insect collects its food it will almost always brush against the flower's pollinating mechanisms. Bees and most other insects prefer to stay faithful to one kind of flower at a time, which guarantees a much better rate of cross-pollination. Man exploits many aromatic herbs and garden plants, including trees. Sweet olive is a highly aromatic shrub or small tree of America's Deep South, where it is planted around galleries and verandahs for its fragrance.

This wild honeysuckle, *Lonicera ciliosa*, has a tubular shape, ideally suited to the long tongues of both butterflies and moths. These insects keep their tongues coiled up when not in use. Many of the honeysuckles, especially the climbing varieties, are festooned with highly scented flowers.

Dried freesia petals can be added to a pot-pourri, so that their subtle colours and distinctive fragrance can be enjoyed even when the florets are past their best.

Lilies, such as this stunning *Lilium michiganense*, combine beauty with a wonderful heady scent, guaranteed to attract insect pollinators.

As insects collect nectar, they will pick up pollen from the loaded anthers, which are clearly visible here.

Perfumed flowers, even if small and insignificant, have a distinct advantage over unperfumed ones. These freesia hybrids have the best of both worlds, being both scented, brightly coloured and able to reproduce themselves by offsets.

FACT FILE

❑ In early spring, scout bees search for nectar and pollen. On returning to the hive, they communicate to the other bees their 'memory' of the scent and location of the flowers.

❑ In Asia, frangipani is often planted in cemeteries and around houses for its scent.

❑ Butterflies and day-flying moths rely heavily on scent recognition, and 'butterfly' flowers often have stronger perfumes and a tubular shape, ideally suited to the butterfly's long tongue. *Buddleia* - the 'butterfly bush' - attracts many butterflies. Pictured above are a red admiral, a peacock and a tortoiseshell butterfly, all on the same flower. When the flower spikes are fading and turning brown, the individual flower tubes contain really mature nectar on which the butterflies appear to get drunk. At this time, the buddleia does not smell pleasant to the human nose, but is irresistible to a butterfly. A butterfly's feet are 200 times more sensitive than the human tongue and the insect uses its feet to explore food possibilities. It is easily able to distinguish between water and weak sugar solution.

Sweet scents after dark

As dusk begins to fall, flower shapes become less defined, and scented and pale-coloured or white flowers have the advantage, standing out from their surroundings with a luminosity that will ensure insect visitations. *Hesperis matronalis*, dame's violet, has no scent during the day, but in late afternoon its sweet perfume suddenly becomes noticeable and may attract the day-flying hummingbird hawkmoth, which can be seen as a small dark vibrating blur, hovering over the long-tubed flowers. The pyramidal orchid of northern Europe, Africa and western Asia has a sweetish scent by day which changes to a foxy odour at night. By day its scent and rosy-purple colour are attractive to butterflies and at night its smell attracts nocturnal moths. The flow of the nectar is controlled by the shape of the flower and can only be taken very slowly. The insect's proboscis is guided precisely by two ridges, the guideplate, on the lower petal, or labellum, and while the insect is taking its food, the orchid's paired pollinia - 'blobs of pollen' - have attached themselves to its tongue by means of a sticky 'saddle'. The viscous substance or 'glue' on the underside of this needs a little while to set firm, hence the enforced delay. Eventually the insect leaves with the pollinia adhering firmly to its proboscis and flies to another plant, where pollination takes place. Sometimes, insects have as many as five pairs of pollinia on their 'tongues'.

Dame's violet, or sweet rocket, *Hesperis matronalis*, has white, lilac or mauve flowers that give off a sweet scent towards evening. Moths are attracted to the pale colours, which show up at night.

48

The garden phlox, *Phlox paniculata*, has a gentle fragrance by day and is pollinated by butterflies and other long-tongued insects. At dusk, its scent becomes stronger and moths are attracted to the flowers.

❏ The South American cruel plant, *Araujia sericofera*, is aptly named. It has fragrant white flowers that attract hovering night-moths. They insert their tongues only to find that they are very firmly caught by this appendage. The flower has evolved an effective mechanism that attaches its pollen masses so firmly to the tongue of a visiting moth that only a strong insect can pull away. A weaker moth will flutter vainly all night, attempting to escape; by morning its strength will be exhausted and it will be dead, hanging by its tongue from the flower. A stronger insect may survive until the sun rises and, as the flower expands, it finally releases its prisoner.

The heavy, dangling flowers of datura, or angel's trumpets, have little daytime fragrance, but by evening their musky scent becomes more powerful, attracting night-flying visitors.

The waxflower, *Hoya carnosa*, has thick-petalled, almost artificial-looking pink or white fragrant flowers in a dome-shaped pendulous umbel. They manufacture so much nectar that in an insectless environment, such as in a conservatory, they drip syrup. The waxflower is a climbing vine that can grow to 6m(20ft). The plant starts to bloom after about two years, and then produces many clusters of flowers.

❏ Tobacco flowers, *Nicotiana affine* (above) hang closed and limp during the day, but towards evening they expand and begin to disseminate their fragrance, attracting moths to the flowers. The larger, sturdier *Nicotiana sylvestris* has no daytime fragrance, but a really powerful night scent.

Evil-smelling flowers

The very different scents, smells and odours, stinks and stenches emanating from some plants act as an irresistible lure to pollinating insects other than bees. *Arum conophalloides* is a robust-looking spathe-bearing plant from Turkey with a 30cm(12in) green spathe that shades to a pale mauve inside. The cone-shaped spadix attracts bloodsucking female midges, because the flowers give off a smell exactly like the animals on which the midges normally feed. There are several kinds of *Stapelia*, an African succulent with large, fleshy, five-pointed flowers that may measure as much as 45cm(18in) across. The hairy flowers of *Stapelia nobilis* appear purplish and although carrion flies usually prefer yellowish flowers, when they can smell what appears to be putrescence, they change this preference to purplish-brown, which resembles decaying meat. Another curious succulent, *Caralluma retrospiciens*, has spiny, four-sided combination leaves and stems, topped with spherical heads of fleshy, five-petalled, evil-smelling purple flowers that are fly-pollinated. In quite a different family of plants, the parasitic *Rafflesia* produces male and female flowers that give off a mighty stench of rotting meat as soon as they are ready for visitors. This giant flower, almost funguslike in texture, is pollinated by flies and beetles in the tropical jungles of Southeast Asia. The enormous 'petals' are, in fact, sepals and considered part of the calyx. (The astounding flowers of *Rafflesia* are featured on pages 36 and 99.)

Dracunculus vulgaris, the dragon arum, is not for the faint-hearted. When the huge crimson-purple spathes unfold, the garden will be completely pervaded for at least three days by a smell like an uncleaned abattoir. The flowers attract all types of blowfly, which buzz around the flowers, apparently savouring the odour and seemingly in no hurry to enter the spathe. In cold weather the flowers last longer because the smell does not travel so far, but on hot days it is powerful enough to carry for long distances. Once pollinated, the spathes quickly collapse and the surrounding air regains its former freshness.

Lysichiton americanum, from western North America and eastern Asia is aptly called the skunk cabbage. It has wide butter-yellow spathes, about 30cm(12in) long, which release a very unpleasant odour as they unfurl. After pollination, the spathe breaks off as the spadix lengthens.

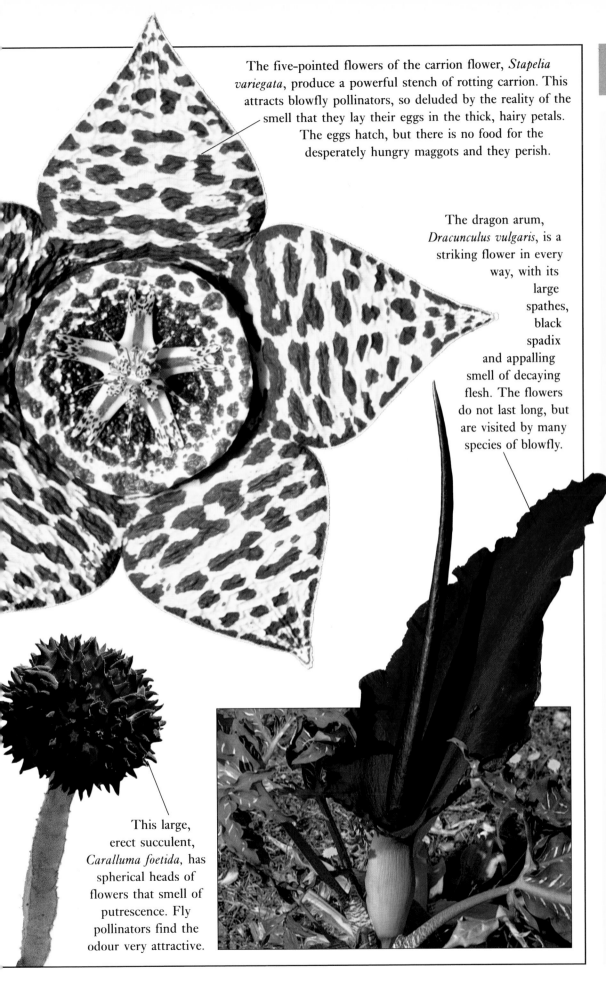

The five-pointed flowers of the carrion flower, *Stapelia variegata*, produce a powerful stench of rotting carrion. This attracts blowfly pollinators, so deluded by the reality of the smell that they lay their eggs in the thick, hairy petals. The eggs hatch, but there is no food for the desperately hungry maggots and they perish.

The dragon arum, *Dracunculus vulgaris*, is a striking flower in every way, with its large spathes, black spadix and appalling smell of decaying flesh. The flowers do not last long, but are visited by many species of blowfly.

This large, erect succulent, *Caralluma foetida*, has spherical heads of flowers that smell of putrescence. Fly pollinators find the odour very attractive.

❏ *Sauromatum venosum*, the voodoo lily, originally from Southeast Asia and tropical Africa, is often sold as a botanical curiosity because it will flower on a windowsill, apparently needing no soil, pot or water. At flowering time, the elongated, lizard-spotted spathes emerge from the corms and elongate to about 60cm(24in), attracting all the flies in the neighborhood into the house. If these can be shut out, the interesting flowers will last much longer - and so will the organic smell.

❏ The pineapple plant, *Eucomis bicolor*, looks rather like a pineapple, with its tuft of bracts at the top. The purple-bordered green flowers begin to emanate a strong, hot smell as soon as they open, most attractive to blowflies, which buzz lazily around the plant.

❏ The skunk cabbage, *Symplocarpus foetidus*, from North America, northeastern Asia and Japan, has hooded yellow-green spathes, spotted and streaked with crimson and purple. As its common name suggests, it smells strongly of skunk when it is ready for pollination in early spring.

❏ *Brachystelma barberae* has a huge storage tuber from which both the foliage and the inflorescence spring briefly into life in its desert habitat in South Africa. It produces interesting and evil-smelling lanternlike purplish flowers, which attract fly pollinators.

Insect traps – a means to an end

Some flowers have evolved into ruthlessly effective insect traps to ensure pollination. *Aristolochia* is a twining climber from Assam and Nepal, with siphon-shaped flowers that act as traps to pollinating flies. Most of its evil-smelling flowers are near ground level, so that their odour remains undisturbed by air currents. The plant is not insectivorous and its pollinators are free to fly away at any time. The cuckoo-pint, or wild arum, from Europe imprisons carrion flies that alight on the spathe, enticed by the smell from the cluster of tiny flowers on the spadix. They crawl downwards, pushing past a ring of downward-pointing hairs, then crawl or fly about in their prison, becoming well coated with pollen. When the hairs wither after pollination, the hungry insects escape, only to visit another nearby arum awaiting pollination. *Nymphaea citrina*, a yellow water lily from Central Africa, has flowers that open as females with immature anthers pointing upward that make a slippery landing site for insects, which slide down into a 'bowl' full of a thin syrup. In the male stage, the bowl dries out and new visiting insects collect pollen from the ripening stamens and fly away unhindered. If they visit a female flower next they will shed their pollen onto the stigmas as they slide downwards.

The stigma and the stamens are located at the base of the flower, hidden deep within the convoluted shape created by the petals. Insects have a long journey to pollinate the flower.

Aristolochia ringens, commonly known as the pelican flower in its native South America, is one of a family of about 350 species. They vary widely in their colour, shape and size.

A cross-section through an *Aristolochia* flower, showing the small insects that seem content to remain inside and lay their eggs, from which grubs hatch.

The section shows the interior of the wild arum. Visiting flies crawl in past the downward-pointing bristles, and while imprisoned they bump against the male flowers directly below the bristles, collecting pollen on their bodies in the process. When the bristles wither, the pollen-coated flies escape and cross-pollinate wild arum plants with receptive stigmas.

Arrow-shaped leaves precede the appearance of the white or purple spathe that encloses the unpleasant smelling flowers of the wild arum.

❏ *Coryanthes*, the bucket orchid, an epiphyte found in Venezuela, is an extraordinary example of an insect-trapping flower. The 'lip' of the flower is shaped like a bucket into which drips a watery secretion from two horns. While the 'bath' is filling, the flower generates a scent that pollinators find irresistible, and when all is ready, the petals and sepals open. A bee flies to the edge of the lip, trying to reach the source of the scent and, intoxicated by the fumes, falls into the slippery-sided bucket, now partly full of water. The bee struggles around in this bath, unable to climb out and unable to fly out because its wings are wet. On the point of drowning, it discovers an escape passage through which it crawls, exhausted and still inebriated, collecting the pollen masses on its body. There is an obstruction in the roof of the passage that prevents the bee from escaping and, by now very tired, it takes some time to gather enough strength to force its way out to freedom - and another bucket orchid. The production of perfume ceases once the insect is trapped, so that by the time the exhausted bee finally leaves, the alluring scent has disappeared, and there is no danger of the insect returning to the same flower, which would then be self-pollinated. After a few hours, the orchid resets its trap to attract further bees, some of which may cross-pollinate the flower.

Mimics among flowers

Many orchid species mimic insects, such as bees, bumblebees and flies, in order to become pollinated. The male insect is attracted to the flower by a series of lures. First, he detects the apparent scent of the 'female' downwind; secondly, he sees what he 'thinks' is a female, as it is the same shape and colour, and finally he is excited by feeling the 'female' lookalike flower, which has hairs of similar length and disposition as a genuine female insect. As he tries to mate with the flower, the pollinia, paired waxy masses of pollen grains, are dislodged and become attached to his neck, whereupon he flies off and carries out the same process with another flower, thus effecting cross-pollination.

The paired pollen masses – called pollinia – are clearly visible.

The flowers of the rare late spider orchid, *Ophrys fuciflora*, resemble fat spiders, but European species are pollinated by male bees of the genus *Eucera tuberculata*.

The slate-blue patch on the lip of the mirror orchid, *Ophrys speculum*, resembles folded insect wings, edged with a fringe of realistic reddish black hairs. The male fly, *Trielis ciliata*, seeing what he thinks is a female at rest on the flower, attempts to mate with her. He is further deceived by the scent of the flower which, it is thought, smells exactly like a female of his species. The yellow orchid, *Ophrys lutea*, is pollinated by male bees of the species *Andrena senecionis*, which alight on the lip backwards, because the markings look like a resting bee facing outwards. The pollinia then become attached to the tip of the bee's abdomen and are transferred to the stigma on the next flower it visits. The stigmatic surfaces of the yellow orchid's flowers are arranged in such a way that they collect the pollinia from the bee's furry abdomen, rather than from its head. In Ecuador, two orchids, *Oncidium planilabre* and *O. hyphaematicum*, have sprays of small black and yellow flowers that resemble a cloud of aggressive male bees of the genus *Centris*. Male *Centris* bees have been seen to attack the flowers and in doing so, the pollinia become attached to the bee's head. When it attacks another flower on another plant, it does so in the same way, aiming at the same part of the flower and driving the pollinia into just the right place to effect pollination.

The fly orchid, *Ophrys muscifera*, looks very like a fly, but is pollinated by the male wasp *Gorytes mystaceus*, which attempts prolonged pseudocopulation with the flowers until the female wasps emerge.

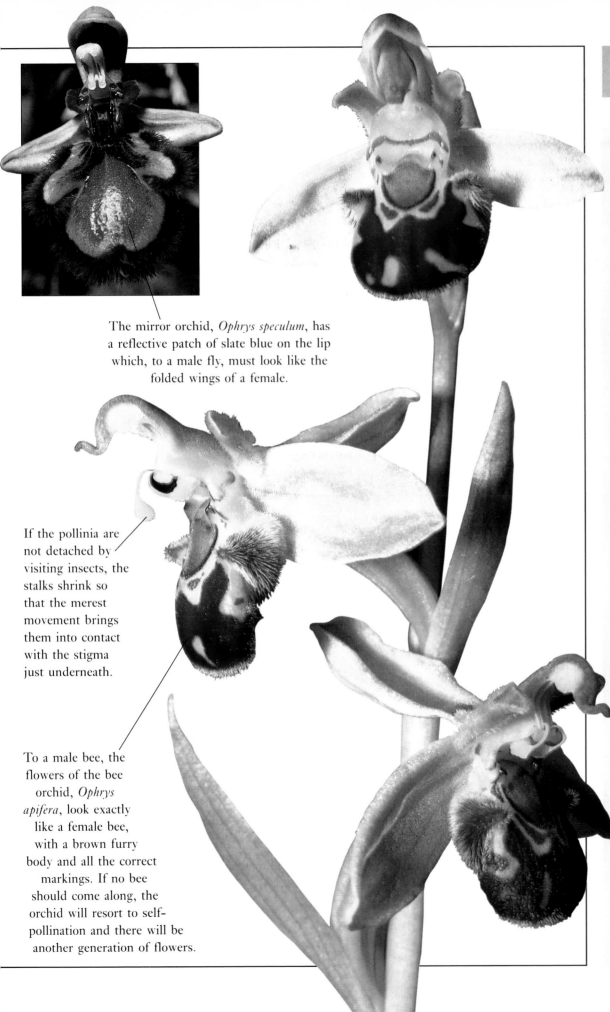

The mirror orchid, *Ophrys speculum*, has a reflective patch of slate blue on the lip which, to a male fly, must look like the folded wings of a female.

If the pollinia are not detached by visiting insects, the stalks shrink so that the merest movement brings them into contact with the stigma just underneath.

To a male bee, the flowers of the bee orchid, *Ophrys apifera*, look exactly like a female bee, with a brown furry body and all the correct markings. If no bee should come along, the orchid will resort to self-pollination and there will be another generation of flowers.

❏ The flowers of a West African myrtle, *Guiera senegalensis*, are often approached by a male digger wasp, *Tacysphex*, which attemps to mate with them.

❏ In the hills of Central America there is an orchid called *Tricheros antennifera* that flowers at the same time as the climbing hempweed. The hempweed produces large quantities of nectar, enjoyed by many other insects and in particular by a parasitic fly that spends its life eating, drinking nectar and copulating. The female flies, sated with sweetness, sit and wait for passing male flies, indicating that they are ready to mate by opening and closing their genitalia. The flowers of the orchid look exactly like the expectant females, with yellow and red-brown markings on the lip, lobes that look like wings, and stiff, glistening abdominal hairs. The male fly descends at speed onto the 'ladies in waiting', but realizes his mistake too late. His brush with romance means that the orchid's pollinia become attached to his abdomen, and when he visits the next flower in exactly the same impetuous way, pollination is achieved as he leaves the pollinia behind.

❏ In order for the mimicry to be successful, it is vital that orchids 'pretending' to be female insects are in flower before the real females are available, otherwise the males will not be interested.

Everlasting flowers

Dried *Banksia* flowerheads are firm and strong. Pick them when the inflorescence looks like an acorn in its cup, and the styles are about one-third open as here.

Some plants have evolved a strategy of appearing to be dead, so that grazing animals leave them alone when they hear these 'everlasting flowers' rustle. Statice, or sea lavender, *Limonium sinuatum*, has bunched flowers of many colours - lavender, violet-blue, pink, carmine, salmon, yellow and orange. The dry calyces retain their natural shapes and most of their colours indefinitely, and the stems are stiff enough when dried not to need wiring. Another member of the family, pink pokers, *Statice suworowii*, has closely packed flower stems that often grow into interesting sinuous curves, and can be wired to dry that way. Annual strawflowers, *Helichrysum bracteatum*, have everlasting flowers in all shades of yellow, orange and red. Occasionally, dark crimson, white and pink appear in packets of mixed-colour seeds. There are tall and dwarf varieties, but all have crisp, papery petals that retain their form and colour for many years. Cut the flowers before they are fully open, while the petals are still incurved over the central disk. Tie them in small bunches and hang them upside down in a cool, darkish, airy place: if dried in bright sunlight they become too brittle.

Banksias have dense flowerheads ideal for drying: some of them, such as *B. serrata*, may have as many as 1,000 flowers in an inflorescence. The flowers take some weeks to open fully, during which time the emerging styles form a contrasting zone and the nectar attracts birds as well as pollinating insects. Bells of Ireland, or shell-flowers (*Moluccella*), have small scented white flowers surrounded by a firm green calyx shaped like a mussel shell. When the flowers are over, the calyces remain, but cut the stems while the flowers are in bloom and the calyces are at their greenest.

The mophead hydrangeas, *Hydrangea macrophylla*, dry very easily and the white varieties are excellent as filler material. Cut the flowerheads when they are still white or wait until they fade to green and they will keep their colour.

Statice is a very useful standby for flower arrangers. It comes in a range of colours and lasts for ever. The dry calyces retain their shape and natural colour and the flower stems are stiff when dried.

The flowers of the annual strawflower come in a large range of bright and soft colours. Pick them before the flowers are fully open. The stems are weak when dried and need wiring straight away.

The flat 'plates' of *Achillea filipendula* dry well when hung upside down and, if picked early enough, retain their pleasing golden yellow for years. The many closely set small flowers will have provided a firm landing platform for pollinating insect visitors.

❑ Globe artichokes, *Cynara scolymus*, have substantial flowerheads with scaly bracts and thistlelike purple florets - so beloved by tired bees in the summer that they spend the night in them. The unopened buds can be dried and, later in the season, also the expanding flowerheads, which will take at least a month to dry properly.

❑ Stand the stems of *Moluccella* (above) in a tall container holding a small amount of water, which will evaporate: allow the stems to dry before arranging them.

❑ *Proteas* can be used fresh in arrangements, but when they begin to fade, stand them in waterless bottles until they are quite dry. If hung, they will close right up, which does not look so attractive.

❑ Almost all the *Alliums* dry well, particularly the ones with spherical flowerheads. Those of *Allium giganteum* measure 15cm(6in) across. All remain faintly onion-smelling.

Century plants

The saguaro cactus, *Carnegia gigantea*, takes about 150 years to grow to an eventual height of 11m(36ft), sometimes more. Young plants mature very slowly and may not flower for 25 years, but eventually the handsome white flowers, with their conspicuous hollow yellow centres, will appear at the tips of the 'arms'. *Welwitschia mirabilis*, from the desert areas of Southwest Africa, is one of the world's most unusual plants. It lives for 100 years or more and in all that time produces only two strap-shaped, leathery leaves that endure for the whole of the plant's life, becoming ever more torn and split at the ends with each succeeding decade in the desert. The leaves continue to grow very slowly from the base all the time to compensate for the attrition. The huge 90cm(3ft)-wide water-storing root protrudes slightly from the ground and in due course, when conditions are right, erect scarlet cones appear bearing single scarlet flowers in the scales. *Puya raimondii* is a gigantic bromeliad from the Peruvian Andes. Some plants are reputed to be 150 years old or more, eventually sending up 12.4m(40ft) flower spikes of greenish white flowers. *Puyas* are able to withstand extreme temperature variability, but they need to be dry. The old-fashioned crimson-flowered peony, *Paeonia officinalis,* is a very long-lived garden plant, reputed to live for 100 years if well cared for. The flowers are nectar-rich and attract many pollinating insects, including beetles.

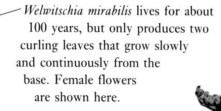

Welwitschia mirabilis lives for about 100 years, but only produces two curling leaves that grow slowly and continuously from the base. Female flowers are shown here.

Puya raimondii, from the Bolivian Andes, normally blooms at about 100 years, though sometimes earlier. It is said to live for up to 150 years.

Agaves, widely known as 'century plants', flowering in Texas. After flowering, the central leaf rosette dies as the seed ripens. New plants come from seed and root suckers.

Yuccas are sometimes confused with agaves and both have been called 'century' plants. Yuccas produce stiff or flaccid leaves, sometimes dangerously spine-tipped.

❏ The yucca is a long-lived plant that thrives in sandy soil in coastal regions. The inflorescence, which does not appear until the plant is several years old, is spectacular, though often produced very late in the year in northern temperate regions. The flowers are 5-7.5cm(2-3in) long, bell-shaped and creamy white in colour.

❏ *Agaves* are plants of hot, dry regions. *Agave americana* is a very characteristic species, with serrated yellow-bordered green leaves, rigid as tree-trunks. These contain large food reserves and eventually, when conditions are exactly right, a majestic 6m(20ft) spike of greenish bells will appear. This may form when the agave is less than 10 years old or the plant may live, flowerless, for 60 years before blooming.

❏ Olive trees, which have wind-pollinated apetalous flowers, may live and bear fruit for 2,000 years or more.

❏ The Sierra redwood, (*Sequoia giganteum*), is not only the tallest tree on earth, but also one of the oldest, with specimens dating to between 3,500 and 4,000 years. Like all conifers, it produces cones. *Pinus aristata*, a bristlecone pine from Nevada, can survive for more than 5,000 years.

❏ Individual baobab trees can live for several thousands of years. They produce pendent 15cm(6in) white flowers.

Moving flowers

Plants do not have a nervous system, but they are capable of movement. Their rudimentary sensitivities can cause reactions to environmental factors, such as light. They can move their leaves or bend their stems (a phenomenon known as 'tropism') and these movements are described as 'tropic'. Movement occurs in leaves, stems and petals that have two surfaces, an upper and a lower or a front and back, and is caused by growth variations in the length of either surface. In a lean-to greenhouse or on a windowsill where seedlings are not regularly turned, for example, the variations consist of progressive stages of non-reversible growth. The seedlings grow towards the light because the concentration of a hormone builds up in the unlit side of the stem and causes it to grow longer than the illuminated one. But consider a bunch of tulips bought on a cold street corner. Put them in a vase in a warm, sunny room and what happens? The stems develop sinuous curves and the petals open right out until the flowers look like water lilies. Put them back into cool dark conditions and they will (more or less) regain their original shapes. This is called a 'nastic' movement and is brought about by a sudden change in light and temperature, which results in the alternate swelling and shrinkage of cell groups that are partially filled with water. Unlike tropism, nastic movement is generally temporary.

The dazzling californian poppy, *Eschscholtzia californica*, has only four petals, which open widely towards the sun, but close when it is cloudy and rainy. They last only two days before falling off.

A field of sunflowers, all following the sun as it moves across the sky during the day. Keeping their 'faces' to the sun ensures that the flowers mature, are pollinated and ripen their seeds.

❑ Darwin did experiments showing that the apex of a plant (when young) recognizes the light stimulus, but does not react to it. The stimulus is then conducted down through the plants' system to the tissues at the base, where the bending generally begins. The apex or tip of the plant produces growth hormones called 'auxins', that move through the tissues to the lower part of the stem and generate growth in that area. If the apex is unevenly lit, less auxin is made available on the lighter side than on the darker side.

❑ The giant sunflower, *Helianthus annuus*, is particularly phototropic, i.e. it grows positively in response to light. It turns to the east each day and then the 25cm(10in) head follows the sun across the sky until, by sunset, the flower face is looking in the opposite direction. At night, the stems slowly return to their original positions until the flowers are ready for the dawn. The individual sunflowers in a row will move at slightly different speeds, but generally follow the same track.

❑ Another flower that follows the sun round is one of the aptly named sundews, *Drosera cistiflora*, an insectivorous plant that lives in damp places throughout South and Southwest Africa. A group of the red or pink saucer-shaped flowers looks most attractive, all gazing simultaneously up at the sun.

Mountain flowers

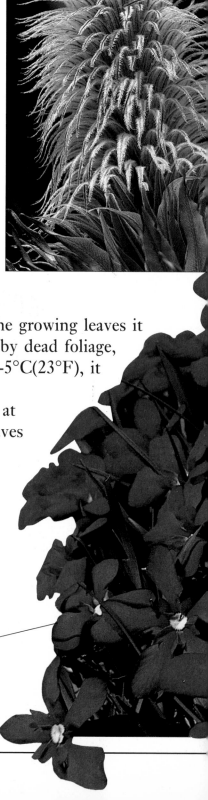

Mountain flowers have adapted to the daily rigours of life in the clouds – summer heat by day and extreme cold by night, sometimes with rain, hail and snow. The giant lobelias of Mount Kenya in Africa have developed an excellent method of coping with temperatures that can fluctuate in one day from 12°C(54°F) down to -6°C(-21°F), which causes the topsoil to freeze. *Lobelia telekii*, for example, looks like a very hairy old man clothed in long silver fur. In fact, the 'fur' is made up of leaves that insulate the growing tip of the plant by a difference of 6°C(11°F). As the plant reaches its full height of 1.8m(6ft), the bracts continue to provide insulation, giving the plant and its emerging flowers a further degree or two of protection. One of the 'tree daisies' of Mount Kenya, *Senecio brassica*, has warm woolly undersides to its leaves to protect the yellow flowers from the otherwise fatal night temperatures. Another, *Senecio keniodendron*, closes its large leaves around the flower shoot at night. Temperature measurements of the plant showed the outside temperature to be as low as -4°C(25°F), while within the shelter of the growing leaves it was 1.7°C(35°F). The stem was similarly protected by dead foliage, so that when the outside temperature was down to -5°C(23°F), it was 2.8°C(37°F) inside the tissues.

The Hawaiian silversword grows in volcanic ash at altitudes of 1,550-3,720m(5,000-12,000ft) and its leaves form a spherical silver cage around the base of the flowering stem with its nodding maroon and yellow 'daisies'. The leaves and stems are covered with shining silver hairs that discourage crawling insects from reaching the flowers – flying insects being more effective cross-pollinators.

The Hawaiian silversword may produce up to 500 flowering heads, and the inflorescence can reach a height of 1.5-1.8m(5-6ft) between June and October. Its stalk is hollow at the base.

After the winter snows of the high Alps have melted, many flowers appear, such as this spring gentian, with its brilliant blue flowers marked with strongly contrasting white nectar guides.

An emerging flower bud of *Lobelia wollastonii*, showing the long, hairy bracts that protect it from the freezing cold of night, when the temperature can drop to a mere 1°C(34°F).

The delicate flowers of *Primula farinosa* bloom as the ice melts. In winter, the plant dies back to a resting bud that begins to grow beneath the snow as the days lengthen.

❏ The *Saussurea* grows at altitudes of 5,270m(17,000ft) in India, Bhutan and Tibet, forming a solid, clumpy plant completely covered in 'hair' through which the purple flowers peer. Delicate-looking *Primulas*, on the other hand, seem able to survive similar extreme fluctuations in temperature without any protection whatsoever.

❏ Edelweiss, *Leontopodium alpinum,* (above) is found high in the European Alps. The whole plant is protected from the cold by dense white wool, which also helps to prevent the evaporation of moisture and accounts for the plant's other common name, flannel flower. In the wild, edelweiss produces a plateau of flowerheads, which pollinating insects can easily cross in their search for nectar.

❏ Hawaiian silverswords die after flowering and fruiting. Their numbers are threatened by the ravages of moth larvae, which have destroyed large quantities of seed.

Polar flowers

The flagellate saxifrage flowers further north than any other arctic plant. The very small leaf rosettes minimize its exposure to the hostile elements. To ensure propagation, it produces daughter plantlets in addition to setting seed.

The Arctic represents a huge landmass capable of supporting plant life, but in this harsh and savage environment, only the hardiest will survive. The shape and texture of the vegetation have adapted to the conditions. The yellow flowers of the arctic cinquefoil, for example, look almost exactly like its European counterpart, except that the plant has developed a hairy, silky coat to protect it from the intense cold of spring nights and the burning rays of the arctic sun. The marsh violet, *Viola palustris*, is found throughout Europe and as far south as Morocco and the Azores, but it is another highly adaptable plant, growing as far north as Greenland and northern Eurasia. It sets seed in the usual way if pollinating insects are about, but also produces seed from another set of self-pollinating flowers, as do other violas and violets. The ubiquitous fireweed, or rosebay willow-herb, is also found in the far north, seldom growing more than 10cm(4in) high, miniaturized by the arctic conditions. It, too, is a born survivor; the opening flowers avoid self-pollination by producing stamens first, with the style and closed stigmas curled round out of the way. When the stamens wither, the style erects and the stigmas open. Polar chickweed, *Cerastium regellii*, grows only in the Arctic circle, forming loose mats of light green leaves dotted with white flowers.

The arctic poppy is circumpolar in distribution. The flowers grow on short hairy stems.

In the southern Indian Ocean, the Kerguelan cabbage grows on Kerguelan Island, from sea level to 620m(2,000ft). It is usually apetalous, though occasional pink or white petalled flowers may appear. Few flying insects can survive the conditions and this rare plant is presumed to be wind pollinated. The same island is home to the rare *Lyallia kerguelensis*, which forms distinctive spreading clumps of compact tufts topped with small whitish flowers. *Astelia pumila*, from the Falklands and southern Chile, is a tiny 'lily' with tussocky, hairy leaves, well designed to protect the slightly scented, pale mauve flowers that hide among them.

The purple saxifrage is an adaptable little plant that produces rose-purple flowers on the exposed cliffs and ridges of the most northerly promontories of arctic Greenland, where few other plants flower. *Sagina caespitosa*, also found in Greenland, Iceland, northern Norway and Sweden, produces tiny tussocks with minute white flowers in summer. The plant is less than 3.2cm(1.25in) high.

The moss campion is found throughout the Arctic and on European mountains as far south as Spain. These low-growing little cushion plants protect themselves by huddling together and retaining their dead leaves as insulation. Further north, the flowers only appear on the south side of the plant.

❏ Grasses and sedges have adapted to the harsh climate of the polar regions, as have some members of the lily tribe and at least one orchid.

❏ *Draba crassifolia* is found in sheltered valleys and ravines, where it is covered by late-melting snows until its small yellow-green flowers appear.

❏ *Androsace triflora*, with three yellow flowers to each stem, is another tiny and beautiful cushion plant found in the arctic wastes of Asia.

❏ *Gunnera magellanica* has attractive leaves and dioecious apetalous flowers that seem to be wind pollinated. It grows in the Falklands, Tierra del Fuego and the Andes.

❏ The mountain avens, *Dryas octopetala*, (above) has compact ground-hugging mats of silver-backed dark leaves and eight-petalled white flowers like small single roses. It is found in mountainous regions throughout Europe, but has adapted to the conditions of Arctic Eurasia, Greenland and Alaska.

Grasses - miniature florets

Grasses are the largest and most important of the plant families, with about 10,000 species distributed throughout the world. They vary in size from very small to the largest of bamboos, which are used to make bridges and houses - not bad for grasses! Most grasses are wind pollinated and produce tiny, very light seeds that will be borne on the wind. Grass flowers develop in clusters - usually compound clusters - and are called florets. When the flowers are ready for fertilization, the cluster expands and pairs of dry, chaffy bracts called glumes begin to separate, exposing the elongating spikelets, which may have anything from one, two or many florets, depending on the type of plant. Each floret has two kinds of bract - a lemma and a palea. The inner parts of the floret expand and are exposed for only a short time each day. The lemma and the palea are pushed apart by two small rounded growths called lodicules, found at the base of the single pistil. The stamens grow up between the lodicules, with slender filaments and long anthers that extend loosely outwards to catch the wind, which carries away their pollen. Usually, grass florets have only three stamens, but bamboos have six or more. The pistil generally has two diverging styles and two long feathery stigmas extending outwards between the two bracts to collect the wind-borne pollen. Only one seed develops in each floret. Grass pollen is very smooth, unlike the textured pollen of most other plants. Some grasses do not rely on wind pollination, but pollinate themselves within the unopened floret. Wheat is just one example.

An enlarged view of wild oat, *Avena fatua*, showing the structure of the florets.

Palea
Anthers
Stigma

Glume
(outer bract)

Lemma
(inner bract)

Awn
(elongated bristle on outer bract)

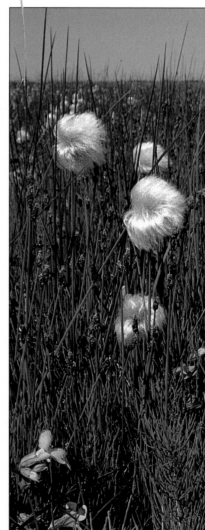

The small flowers, or florets, are enclosed by pairs of glumes, grouped singly, in pairs or in small groups within another pair of bracts or scales. The spikelets can be arranged in various ways - stalkless, in spikes or with long-stalked branched flowers, as here in cocksfoot grass.

Cortaderia selloana is a fine ornamental pampas grass. The plumes of female plants are much larger and silkier than those of the males.

Cotton grass in Alaska. The primitive grasses adapted to wind- or self-pollination and began to dominate prairies. Vast populations of grasses flourished in all habitats, from tropical plains, savannas, marshes, forests and deserts, to temperate steppes and on mountains.

❏ Grasses first began to appear about 20 million years ago. They are the largest group of monocotyledons (i.e. plants having one seed leaf in the embryo) and are the principal plants of all the prairie-like areas of the world. Their hardiness and adaptability are due in part to the fact that a monocot leaf is able to continue growing from its base if the tip is damaged. This is why cutting grass with a lawnmower does the plant no harm at all. Its parallel veins close off at the damaged area of the leaf and the plant grows up from the base.

❏ Bamboos flower very occasionally, with graceful spikelets appearing on the same species of plants simultaneously all over the world. After this flowering the plants apparently die, but new growth does eventually appear from the roots, although it takes many years to regenerate new plants. The giant of the bamboo tribe is *Dendrocalamus giganteus*, which achieves a height of 30m(100ft) in less than three months, growing at a rate of 90cm(36in) in 24 hours.

❏ It has been estimated that there are about 620 genera and 10,000 species of grass.

❏ Bermuda grass, *Cynodon dactylon*, is the commonest and most widely distributed grass, being found in Canada, Argentina, New Zealand, West and South Africa and Japan.

Life in the canopy

Up in the tree canopy of jungles and rainforests there is another layer of plants. This is a realm dominated by epiphytic plants - ones that cling onto other plants, but only for support so that they can spread their leaves to catch all the light - and in some cases the rainwater - that filters down through the trees. Among these plants are many stunning bromeliads and orchids that make their homes on trunks and tree branches. Bromeliad leaves usually grow in the form of rosettes to retain rainwater that in turn provides a supply of water and dissolved nutrients to keep the plant alive. Epiphytic orchids support themselves on a tree with strong whitish roots that can absorb and store nutrients and moisture. To help them survive, epiphytic orchids have developed a two-way relationship with certain fungi. The minute orchid seed must make contact with this fungi, which will start it into growth and support it in its early stages. It can penetrate the orchid root and gives the orchid organic nourishment derived from the humus in and on the tree bark. It also takes its own form of nourishment from the orchid, which in turn is capable of absorbing the fungus, in this way keeping the relationship stable. Some climbers are able to hoist themselves up to the canopy by means of tendrils or their own twining stems. Many tropical species have year-round bloom. The jade vine from the Philippines is a lusty jungle vine with pendent racemes of an unusual blue-green colour, rare among flowering plants. It grows to a height of 25m(80ft) and its dangling stems may carry as many as 100 long-lasting blossoms, often used in garlands.

This bromeliad, *Neoregelia carolinae*, from South America is called a 'tank epiphyte' because it has developed watertight leaf bases as reservoirs in order to collect and hold rainwater. Some of these reservoirs support whole colonies of creatures, such as mosquito and dragonfly larvae, snails, slugs, lizards and frogs. The tiny lilac flowers arise in the centre of the rosette.

In the warm, moist atmosphere of the tropical forest, bromeliads can send up colourful flower spikes at any time of year. The real flowers are small in relation to the bracts from which they spring.

This *Tillandsia* from tropical America is a rootless bromeliad, a true 'air plant' that lives on the nutrients in moist air. These plants make their homes on branches and tree trunks, using their roots as anchorages only and not to take nourishment from their host.

Petrea volubilis is also known as the sandpaper vine, because of the roughness of the leaves. The paler 'flower' is really the calyx, which lasts indefinitely, while the real violet-coloured flowers are in the centre. These fall off after only a day or so.

❏ When they are about to flower, the inner surfaces of some bromeliad leaves change colour, harmonizing or contrasting with the bracts or flowers; the whole inflorescence makes a brilliant splash of colour in the treetops and is more easily seen by pollinators. After flowering, the leaves lose their glow.

❏ The 'urn' bromeliads support colonies of other creatures in their reservoirs, from micro-scopic organisms to insects and even frogs (above).

❏ *Akebia* is a vigorous vine, climbing sideways or upwards to great heights in the canopy by means of its twining stems, with which it can strangle and suffocate a host plant or tree. In warm regions it is evergreen, but in temperate areas it may lose its attractive leaves in hard winters. With its dangling 2.5cm(1in) racemes of heavily scented, dark crimson flowers, this is an excellent semi-evergreen to grow for the quick concealment of unsightly buildings. Male and female flowers are separate, but are found on the same stem.

Seaside flowers

Some plants can tolerate - and even seem to need - a degree of salinity in the soil, though in excess, salt is harmful to plants. The graceful tamarisk, for example, is part of the coastal scene in many parts of the world, with its feathery light green branches and pink flowers. The small scalelike leaves are well able to resist strong, salt-laden winds and, although the slender racemes of pink flowers appear delicate, they are quite able to withstand adverse maritime conditions. In fact, the tamarisk is so well adapted to a strong saline content in the soil that it does not always thrive away from the coast. One problem for saltwater plants is getting enough water into their roots. Fresh water normally flows into the tiny root hairs of a plant by osmosis because the concentration of salts is stronger inside the plant tissues than it is in the film of water clinging to the outside surface of the root. Plants that literally 'sit' in a relatively strong salt solution get over this problem by maintaining an even stronger concentration of salts in their root hairs than in their surroundings. Conserving water is another strategy for seaside plants. It is very common for seaside plants to have reduced leaves, tough cuticles, salt-resistant bark and mechanisms that enable them to resist excessive water loss. Sea kale is a giant plant that forms huge, unmoving, cabbagelike rosettes of leaves, seemingly impervious to sea spray, cutting winds, blown sand and shifting shingle. It is grown as a vegetable, but is now more usually seen as a highly decorative border plant, producing a tall tracery of stems starred with tiny, scented white flowers. It takes three years to flower from seed.

Sea pinks carpet cliff edges, firmly anchoring themselves into rock crannies with long, strong roots to withstand the buffeting of spray-laden, gale-force winds.

Sea holly is well equipped to withstand inclement shoreside conditions, with long, tough roots and strong, leathery, spiny foliage and bracts.

The delicate-looking sea-bindweed, *Calystegia soldani*, grows surprisingly well above high water mark. It is equipped with a very deep rooting system, which enables it to endure constant wind and spray, as well as the constantly shifting shingle.

The horned poppy grows well in the exposed, windy conditions of shingle beds above high water mark. The ruffled leaf rosettes are securely anchored by their long, deep roots.

❏ Plants that can live in soils kept moist or permanently wet by salt water are called halophytes (from the Greek *halos*, meaning 'sea salt'). Their cell tissues are not destroyed by salt solutions; indeed some halophytes, such as *Limonium vulgare*, thrive in saline habitats. Other plants might not be exposed to submergence by sea water, but can withstand being regularly doused by sea spray. Another large group of plants, the xerophytes (from the Greek *xeros*, meaning 'dry'), can establish themselves in mobile sand. Most have unusually deep or wide-spreading root systems and can withstand burial by loose sand and shingle. Marram grass, *Ammophilia arenaria*, is often planted to stabilize shifting dunes, establishing a network of anchoring roots and stems inside the dunes.

❏ *Lathyrus japonicus*, the summer-flowering beach pea (above) grows on coastal shingle and along the shores of the Great Lakes in the USA. Similar pea flowers are found on beaches around the world.

Water lilies and lotus flowers

Water plants spread very quickly by means of fleshy, creeping roots and shoots and many also set seed, which is dispersed by the surrounding water. The royal, or giant, water lily (*Victoria regia*) is one of the wonders of the plant world. In the quiet waters of its native Amazon, the bud opens in the morning and by late afternoon the flower is fully extended, remaining open all night. The flowers measure 30cm(12in) across, and there may be 60 or more white petals shading to rose and purple in the centre. Only one flower opens at a time, just above the water surface. The buds, stems, fruits and the undersides of the great leaves are all prickly. The structure of the large leaves has excited students of architecture because of the intricate pattern of ribs and veins that support it. The larger the leaf, the more surface area there is available for photosynthesis to produce energy to make the large flowers. Water plant leaves generally have a tough cuticle, often covered in mucilage, which resists buffeting.

The sacred lotus (*Nelumbo nucifera*) of Asia, with fragrant rose-pink flowers measuring 30cm(12in), is so-called because Buddha is often protrayed seated in a lotus flower. The Ancient Egyptians revered the ordinary water lily (*Nymphaea*), which they called a lotus flower. At funerals, these were traditionally laid in the sarcophagi and have been so well preserved that botanists have been able to identify species that have changed little in 4,000 years.

The flowers of the royal water lily slowly open in the morning, are fully expanded by afternoon and remain open all night. They open one at a time on each plant.

The giant water lily can sometimes grow in water 9m(30ft) deep during a flood, shooting up rapidly to allow for the increased water depth.

The huge leaves of the giant water lily can reach up to 2m (6.5ft) across and are strong enough to support the weight of a child. A network of ribs on the undersurface keeps each leaf rigid, and air trapped in spaces within the leaves ensures that they stay afloat to catch the maximum sunshine each day.

The flowers of most water lilies are open during the day, but begin to close during the afternoon.

Some water lilies bear flowers on long stems above the water, but the flowers of this *Nymphaea* float on the surface.

The sacred lotus from Asia has large, delicately shaded pink flowers. The stems and blooms stand right out of the water. These plants do best in areas of still water, such as shallow lakes, and flower best in sunny surroundings.

❏ Water snowflake (shown below) is often mistaken for a water lily, but actually belongs to the gentian family.

❏ The white blooms of the giant water lily open at dusk and their pineapple scent attracts beetles and other insects. As midnight approaches, the flowers turn a deep shade of reddish purple and the petals close, trapping the beetles. The following evening they open again, freeing the beetles, now coated in pollen to fertilize other flowers nearby.

❏ Water lilies are probably the oldest group of flowering plants. The earliest known fossilized pollen originated from one of these plants about 140 million years ago.

❏ Birds such as the lily-trotters, or jacanas, have elongated toes that enable them to walk across water lily leaves as they stalk insects and small fish that shelter near the lily pads.

73

From the bank into the shallows

River banks, lake shores and shallow fresh waters around the world are home to a wide variety of flowering plants that have adapted to flourish in various depths of water. Splendid among the plants along the banks of northern temperate waters is the yellow flag iris (*Iris pseudacorus*), which raises its large flowers up to 1.8m(6ft) above the water surface. Bees pollinate these flowers by following the dark nectar guides and crawling right into the deep centre of the flower. On its way in, the bee brushes against the stigma and deposits any pollen it has picked up from other blooms. As the bee feeds on the nectar further down the flower, the anthers dust it with a new batch of pollen, with which it can cross-pollinate another flag iris. To prevent self-pollination, the stigma bends out of the way as the bee exits. Among the floating plants, the water soldier (*Stratiotes aloides*), shows a useful adaptation to its watery habitat. During the winter, it remains on the bottom, protected from ice and cold weather, but during the summer the leaf rosette floats up to the surface like a giant spider and produces white flowers on separate male and female plants. Further out from the bank in tropical waters, a floating plant with the common name of water hyacinth (*Eichhornia crassipes*) belies its apparently harmless image.

Despite its attractive flowers and fragile appearance above the water surface, the water hyacinth is a dangerous plant. In dirty, nutrient-rich waters, it rapidly produces rafts of almost indestructible leaves and trailing roots that can choke lakes and waterways and impede navigation. Although native to South America, it has been introduced to tropical waters in many parts of the world, with disastrous results. In Florida, the cost of eradicating it has resulted in its being called 'the million-dollar weed'.

The delicate lilac-blue flowers of the water hyacinth last for only a few hours, but its leaves are tough and unsinkable. They have gas-filled 'buoyancy tanks' that keep the plant afloat. This rapidly growing plant causes congestion in many tropical waterways.

The flowering rush, *Butomus umbellatus*, is not a rush at all, although it has rushlike leaves. It flourishes in slow-moving streams, growing to a stately 1.2m(4ft). The pink flowers have only three petals, a feature common to many water plants.

The yellow flag iris has faintly scented, yellow flowers, with well-defined nectar guides on the petals. Their shape inspired a stylized form of the flower, the fleur-de-lys, used as the emblem of France since the Crusades.

❏ The popular image of 'Moses in the bullrushes' should really be 'Moses in the greater reedmaces', as these are the plants usually depicted.

❏ Some plants flower and are pollinated under water. In hornworts (*Ceratophyllum* sp.), the stamens of the tiny male flowers float up to the surface and release pollen grains that in turn sink very slowly to the bottom, pollinating any female hornwort flowers they encounter on the way.

❏ *Vallisneria*, or tapegrass, lives under water except at flowering time, when the minute female flowers, still attached by their stems, float to the surface, while the male flowers break loose from the parent plant and rise as 1mm(0.04in) stemless buds. On the water surface, the tiny male flowers (above left) open by reflexing their sepals and drift towards the exposed stigmas of the female flowers (above right) to pollinate them. After pollination, the female flower stem has been seen to coil into a spiral that pulls the fertilized flower down to the bottom, where the fruits ripen.

Desert flowers

Many plants have adapted to the aridity and extreme temperature fluctuations of desert conditions. The difference in temperature between day and night in the desert can be as much as 30°C(54°F), so plants must be physiologically fit to survive this potential stress. They have devised a variety of strategies. For example, the coachwhip *(Fouquiera splendens)* conserves energy by shedding its leaves when water is scarce, and its tall, thin, unbranched stems are spiny and cast little shade. However, after rain, the shrub produces a new set of bright green leaves that gradually stiffen into thorny points to deter browsing animals. The stems are only 2.5cm(1in) thick, but they grow to 6m(20ft), with waving clusters of red flowers at the tips. Coachwhips can produce up to seven sets of leaves each year. They are found from California to Mexico, and are known by a number of other common names, including banner cactus, ocotillo and cat's claw. The unique boojum tree *(Idria columnaris)*, another desert dweller, has evolved tapering, carrot-shaped green trunks that act as water reservoirs. During drought, it has short leafless branches, but after rain, leaves and clusters of white flowers quickly appear. When the drought returns, the boojum tree sheds its leaves and ekes out an existence on its water reserves, and its trunks gradually become thinner and thinner until they bend over. In the desert areas of California and Mexico, boojum trees grow to 9m(30ft). In Africa, a succulent known as the ghostman has a similar method of survival, although it is not as tall. The tumbleweed uses a different strategy. After flowering, its branches dry out, the plant forms into a ball, breaks out of the soil and rolls away, scattering seeds as it goes.

Brief rains spawn a carpet of flowers across this semi-desert area 320km(200 miles) southwest of Alice Springs in central Australia, where the annual rainfall is 25cm(10in) or less. These plants – members of the huge daisy family (Compositae) – are able to flower and set seed rapidly.

Once a year in arid parts of Australia, the countryside turns scarlet with the amazing-looking flowers of Sturt's desert pea. The prostrate branches can measure up to 90cm(36in) long, and the elongated scarlet flowers, each with a distinctive black spot at the base, erupt in bunches of four to six. The grey-green leaves are covered with silky silver hairs.

The coachwhip's adaptation to desert conditions is to remain leafless except after rain. The bright red flowers have very prominent stamens.

When the bitterroot's starlike flowers appear, the leaves wither. This desert plant stores water in its fleshy roots, once eaten by American Indians.

❑ The bitterroot hoards precious moisture in its fleshy leaves, roots and buried stems. Although it looks frail, the plant can endure about two years of drought conditions.

❑ The scented white flowers of the pretty desert primrose, (*Oenothera* sp.), shown above, turn pink as they wither.

❑ If you don't want to be eaten, make yourself stink - that's the evolutionary tale of aromatic plants that grow in deserts - or combine vile odours with vicious spines and/or an everlasting habit.

❑ In some desert areas in the southern USA and Mexico, the creosote bush dominates the landscape as far as the eye can see. It has small, twisted yellow flowers and a powerful resinous smell to its leaves that successfully deters animals looking for a meal.

❑ *Agave attenuata* has a strange, curving flower stem and a dedicated attitude towards survival - it produces ripened fruits at the bottom of the flower stem, expanding flowers for pollinating insects and small plantlets at the tip.

Cacti and succulents

The term 'succulents' covers about 10,000 species of flowering plants, including several thousand species of cacti. These plants have adapted very well to life in arid surroundings by storing water in special spongy tissue in stems, leaves or roots. The prickly pear, or 'bunny's ears' (*Opuntia*), for example, thrives in the hot, dry regions of its native southern USA and Mexico, where its jointed shape is characteristic of desert areas. *Opuntia* species have red or yellow flowers with an abundance of stamens and are very attractive to bees. The plants photosynthesize so effectively that young shoots produce 'nectar' from the tips of their spines. The nectar is described as extranuptial, 'outside marriage', as it does not lead to pollination, but is a bonus to passing insects. Ants prefer it to flower-nectar, which is fortunate because, being so small, if they raid the flowers they take the nectar and contribute nothing towards pollination. Among the enormous range of other succulent plants, the 'living stones' (*Lithops*) are particularly fascinating. When not in bloom, these plants are almost impossible to distinguish from the stones of the African deserts. The flowers - yellow or white, but never red - emerge from a cleft between the paired, fleshy leaves. These plants can survive for more than a year without water. The flowers provide a trysting-place for copulating insects, a phenomenon that occurs worldwide, wherever flowers offer suitable accommodation.

Once the flowers die, a new pair of leaves emerges.

Only when the flowers of *Lithops* emerge from the paired leaves is it possible to distinguish this well-camouflaged plant easily from its natural stony desert habitat.

When a large insect lands on the style of this *Opuntia* flower, the stamens rise up around it to form a brush that 'paints' the underside of the insect with pollen.

This
curve-billed
thrasher is just
one of the many
birds and insects that
sip nectar from the saguaro
flowers by day. At night they
are visited by bats and the
long-tongued hawkmoths.
The waxy flowers have
long stamens.

The large, fragrant
flowers of the
hedgehog cactus
have a deep-
centred corolla
surrounded by
stamens that
deposit pollen
on insects.

Opuntia flowers
produce abundant
nectar that attracts a wide
variety of insect pollinators.

❏ *Lithops* are aptly known as 'living stones'. They belong to the Mesembryanthemum family and come from the arid parts of South and Southwest Africa. There are about 70 species, many of them difficult to tell apart, because their upper surfaces have no chlorophyll and therefore no green colour. This upper surface acts as a window, allowing light to pass through the water-retaining storage tissues to the chlorophyll layer at the sides of the plants. In the wild, this layer is buried in sand and stones.

❏ *Conophytum minusculum* is most interesting to grow, as the flower, which lasts for about two weeks, is about twice the size of the plant. After flowering, the plants dry up for a resting period and are then almost impossible to see. It is probable that there are even more species than the 250 already known to science.

❏ The bright reds, magentas and pinks seen in the flowers of cacti and many other succulent plants are produced by a chemical called betacyanin, which is different from the anthocyanin that produces these colours in other plant groups. This explains why many succulent plants have such distinctively coloured flowers. With few exceptions, there are no blue flowers among the succulents.

❏ The giant saguaro cactus can grow over 20m(66ft) tall.

Flowering trees

Trees have an amazing array of glorious flowers, especially tropical giants that flower in the canopy, out of sight, producing marvellous fruits of the forest. Blue flowers are the rarest colour in the plant world and a tree-size mass of them is pure delight. The jacaranda has large, graceful panicles of blue to violet bell-shaped flowers and delicate fernlike foliage. Originally from Brazil and Argentina, it is now seen in all tropical, subtropical and Mediterranean countries, where it is used for street and park planting. Some species may begin to flower at three years old and will eventually grow to 12.4m(40ft). The horse chestnut, *Aesculus hippocastanum*, is a majestic European tree with upright panicles of deep pink or white flower spikes, like Christmas tree candles perched on the ends of the branches. The lowest and largest flower spikes grow out at an angle to catch the light of the sun, and straighten up and taper off in size as they near the top of the tree. *Frangipani* is a small tropical tree growing to 6m(20ft). It has been described as 'a set of antlers decked with posies', because the fragrant waxy flowers appear on bare branches just as the new foliage emerges, but the beauty of its long-lasting rose-pink flowers more than compensates for its angularity. The 'foxglove tree', *Paulownia tomentosa*, found from the eastern Himalayas to western China, has upright panicles of lilac to purple flowers and makes a handsome ornamental tree in subtropical and tropical areas. The flower buds form in autumn and are carried through the winter on bare branches. *Delonix regia* from Madagascar is a spectacular deciduous tree that, while still bare of foliage, begins to produce an exuberance of scarlet flowers, all the more striking because they appear just as the feathery new leaves unfold. They are followed by large seedpods 30cm(12in) long.

The long-lived, scented, trumpet-shaped flowers of frangipani, *Plumeria acuminata*, can be white, yellow, pink or red in colour. They have long been popular for decoration and have been made into perfume. Newly opened petals contain a milky latex, distasteful to browsing animals.

This African tulip tree, *Spathodea campanulata* - no relation to the North American tulip tree, *Liriodendron tulipifera* - is pollinated by sunbirds. If these sharp-beaked birds probe too roughly for nectar, they may be squirted with an evil-smelling juice found in the inflated calyces of the unopened flower buds.

The Australian wattle, *Acacia dealbata*, produces branches of deliciously scented fluffy yellow balls, which are mainly pollen-rich stamens set off by finely cut evergreen foliage. It is often wrongly called mimosa, but the name persists with florists and gardeners. It is not hardy and may be severely damaged by frost.

FACT FILE

❏ The spectacular scarlet blossom of the Australian red-flowering gum, *Eucalyptus ficifolia*, is so abundant that it almost obscures the foliage.

❏ *Firmiana colorata*, from India, Ceylon, Thailand and Sumatra grows to 26m(85ft). It has been described as a glowing fountain of a tree, with racemes of brilliant orange flowers that appear from March until May on bare branches. Male and female flowers grow in separated groups, though they appear on the same branch.

❏ It is easy to forget how beautiful an apple tree is when in full bloom (above) - with flowers from palest pink to the deep cerise of unopened buds. Apiarists often put their hives in orchards while the blossom is out for a better crop of apples - and honey.

❏ *Amherstia nobilis* from Southern Burma grows to only 9m(30ft), with pendulous racemes of light red orchidlike flowers. Seldom seen in the wild now, but a feature of a number of botanical gardens.

The art of plant breeding

For centuries – long before they understood anything about genetics – gardeners and growers selected and then bred from designated plants. It was not until the middle of the nineteenth century that a monk called Gregor Johann Mendel began to study plant heredity. Mendel, a student of many scientific subjects and a mathematician, conducted experiments under controlled conditions with pea flowers – a fortunate choice, as it turned out, because not all flowers would have given such clear-cut results. He discovered that the factors that determined such features as flower colour, height of plant and form of the seedpod in the common pea were quite distinct from each other and transmitted intact from parent to offspring. This clarified the original thinking that characteristics were simply 'mixed' in succeeding generations. His findings laid down the basic ground rules for the 'science of genetics.' Today, plant breeders are always trying to 'improve' colour, size, shape, habit and resistance to disease, or to breed double flowers where only singles previously existed. There are two kinds of double flowers; one has stamens and/or carpels that have mostly changed to petals, and the other double flower is found in members of the large daisy family, or Compositae. These have two sorts of flower in the 'composite' heads – disc florets in the centre and ray florets around the edge. Both may be fertile. In dahlias and chrysanthemums, which have been selectively cultivated for hundreds of years, the flowerheads are composed of outer ray florets only and the disc florets have disappeared.

'Dancia' is a modern dahlia hybrid, a descendant of the species plants first discovered in Mexico at the time of the Spanish Conquest in 1519-1524.

This handsome iris 'Olympic challenge' has to be propagated vegetatively, as its seedlings would not be true. Commercial plant breeding is painstaking and expensive, because it takes many years to produce the new varieties.

Chrysanthemum myconis is a species plant, which means that it is an uncultivated, original plant and its progeny will be exactly the same as the parent flower. Breeding from such species plants has created the huge variety of modern hybrids.

This chrysanthemum belongs to the large group of florists' chrysanthemums, all derived from crosses between *Chrysanthemum indicum* and *C. morifolium*, and from other wild forms native to China and Japan. These hybrids are propagated vegetatively.

❑ Sweet peas (above) began life in Sicily and are first recorded in about 1697, when they were described as having small, powerfully scented red-purple flowers, with only two blooms to a stem. Experiments with their culture proceeded very slowly until the late 19th century, when there was a surge of interest. In 1900, no less than 264 varieties were on show at the great bicentenary Sweet Pea Exhibition and the flowers were beginning to look something like those of today.

❑ Plant-breeders found that orchid seeds could be germinated without the assistance of the symbiotic fungus that occurs in nature, and that plants could be grown on a substitute medium. Orchid seedlings take six to seven years to come to flowering, but the financial rewards are considerable, as orchids can live for many years and each spray can last for months. Hybrid orchids can be cloned by culturing a few cells from the growing tip in a special nutrient medium.

Improving on Nature

Plant breeders now exclude all insects from their carefully controlled glasshouse development areas. They usually remove the petals to facilitate handling and then emasculate the flowers by carefully removing the anthers (which can be labelled and laid aside to be used on other experiments) to prevent self-pollination. When the stigma of the prepared flower is seen to be ready, the chosen pollen is transferred to it and a paper cap or other covering is placed around the pollinated stigma to prevent any additional pollen settling on it. The seedpod will form and ripen and then the seeds must be sown and grown on. In some cases it will be several years before the results are known, and then further selections and crosses will need to be made. Commercial plant breeding is an exceedingly lengthy and costly business and many breakthroughs have been achieved by dedicated amateurs. Pansies and violas, fuchsias, foxgloves, asters, narcissi, primulas, irises, hydrangeas, lilies, dahlias, hyacinths, antirrhinums, pinks, carnations, gladioli and many more have been the subject of genetic engineering, not always for the better. Some flowers, such as the auricula (a type of primula), had keenly supported societies and many shows, but the varieties bred during the last century have not survived and are only known to us from written descriptions or paintings. Other species, including roses and orchids, have strong support from gardeners who take a pride in preserving both old varieties and cultivating new ones.

Viola lutea is one of the forebears of the amazingly coloured modern pansy. The cultivated flowers must be grown in special conditions to produce true seed. Left to themselves, seedlings of the modern hybrids would soon revert.

The first 'pansies' appeared in the later part of the 19th century. They were a cross between *Viola tricolor*, *V. lutea* and probably *V. altaica*.

This frost-tender fuchsia hybrid is very different from the hardier species fuchsias from South America. They began to find their way into cultivation during the latter part of the 18th century and their popularity grew steadily.

When the plant breeder is satisfied that the stigma of the flower is ready, the selected pollen is transferred to it. This tulip is being pollinated with a paintbrush. Once successfully pollinated, the stigmas must be protected from any risk of accidental pollination by insects.

FACT FILE

❏ The early cultivators and growers of flowers were called 'florists'; flower shops as we know them did not exist. Later, the term was applied to people who sold flowers.

❏ Tulips can acquire a virus that is not carried in the seed but is transmitted by aphids. The virus does the tulip no harm, but produces very beautiful 'broken' markings, such as streaks and 'feathers' on second-generation or subsequent flowers. During the sixteenth and seventeenth centuries, some of these flowers became unrealistically valuable and the passion for them was called 'tulipomania', but none have come down to us. However, named varieties of 'Rembrandt' tulips, such as 'Absalon' and 'Maybloom', with two or more colours in the petals, give an idea of how these historic flowers looked.

❏ In 14th-century Europe, pinks and carnations were bred with devotion. We can recognize specific types featured in royal portraits.

The magnificent roses

The first roses were strong and thorny with single flowers. The thorns enabled the stems to climb towards air and sunlight in the forests, and protected the roses from grazing animals on the prairies and grasslands. Single flowers were best, as there were then more anthers – double flowers are usually unable to set seed. In the cooler Northern Hemisphere, roses all flowered in midsummer and many natural hybrids occurred. In warmer regions the flowering period was longer, there were less coincidental flowerings and fewer natural crosses. Initially, roses were cross-pollinated naturally by insects and selected seedlings grown on, but then gardeners began to bring roses from other areas together. The function of pollen began to be understood in the 16th century. The Empress Josephine was a collector of roses, and by 1815 her head gardener was caring for 300 roses, which had begun to produce some interesting progeny. Subsequently, several important rose nurseries were started and the rose breeders, then as now, aimed for new colours, good form, a long flowering season, hardiness and resistance to disease. For a long time, fragrance was not considered vital. The story of one modern rose – 'Peace' – is particularly interesting. Raised in the Meilland nurseries in the South of France in about 1935, this huge, pink-tinged yellow rose was shown to the American ambassador in 1939 and he was so impressed with it that he arranged for budwood – the propagating material – to be sent to America in the diplomatic bag, where stocks were built up by the American rose grower, Conard Pyle. The new rose was christened 'Peace' in 1945 at the end of World War Two.

Wild roses were among the parents of today's amazing hybrids. *Rosa palustris*, shown here, tolerates wet ground, hence its common name of swamp rose. Other species thrive in equally inhospitable conditions; *Rosa acicularis*, the polar rose, tolerates cold; *R. stellata* grows in arid upland areas and *Rosa pimpinellifolia* is found among windblown coastal dunes.

❏ Chinese gardeners were cultivating roses about 1,000 years ago. From the single-flowered, once-blooming climbers they bred many-petalled, repeat-flowering shrubs with fragrant flowers that were later to be crossed with the European roses.

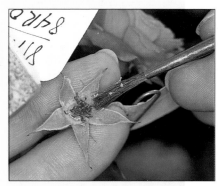

❏ Rose growers produce their stocks vegetatively, by 'budding' onto strong wild briar stocks. Periodically they must go back to seed-producing stock to keep the subsequent progeny healthy. The above rose flower - with its petals removed - is being dusted with pollen from another plant to produce a hybrid.

❏ Breeders have been, and still are, trying to breed a pure blue rose. There are chemical similarities in the pigment that produces magenta (a sharp red) and blue so, theoretically, a blue flower could occur at any time. In many flowers it seems that the pigment that produces magenta can be 'switched' by chemicals in the sap or petals to create a blue colour. Unfortunately, roses do not have the chemicals needed to 'switch' red to blue.

Roses are classified by their growing habit. The 'Peace' rose shown here is a hybrid tea, meaning that the bush has large, single blooms.

In terms of variety of size, shape, colour, scent and habit, few flowers can compete with the rose. This strong rambler, 'Albertine', can climb to 6m(20ft), whereas miniature roses only grow 15-25cm(6-10in) high.

The floribunda is yet another popular form of rose. The flowers are smaller than those of the hybrid tea and grow in clusters. This is the famous 'Molly McGredy' bred in 1968.

Flowers for the pot

The medicinal value of most herb plants lies in their leaves or roots, but in some cases the flowers are used for flavouring or decorating food. One example is the cottager's marigold, its fresh or dried petals add flavour and colour to soups, beef stews, salads, cheese dishes and rice. Cowslips, *Primula veris*, were once used to make a very potent wine, but because of its increasing scarcity the plant is now protected in some parts of the world. Primroses are still candied for cake decoration by steeping gum arabic in water, wetting the flowers with this and then dipping them in caster sugar. The flowers, leaves and seeds of the *Nasturtium* have a pleasantly hot flavour and can be used to garnish salads, while borage has a cool cucumber taste and its flowers and leaves are used to decorate summer drinks and wine cups. The lilac-mauve flowers of thyme are rich in nectar and are good bee-flowers. This low wiry plant covers the slopes of Mount Hymettus in Greece, which has been famous for over 2,000 years for its honey. Thyme flowers are used to flavour soups and stews.

Candied primrose flowers make colourful decorations for a small chocolate cake. Other edible flower petals include roses, violets and geraniums. They can be frozen in ice cubes to float in drinks or to decorate a table.

❑ Tansy, *Tanacetum vulgare*, has golden-yellow buttonlike flowers that used to be gathered to make tansy pudding at the end of Lent. It is a bitter-tasting herb.

❑ The flowers of alkanet, *Pentaglottis sempervirens*, can be added to salads or made into an exciting-looking conserve to accompany game.

❑ Elderflowers, *Sambucus nigra*, (above) can be dipped in batter to make pancakes or broken up to flavour sorbets, desserts and vinegar.

❑ At one time, vast fields of *Rosa officinalis*, the apothecary's rose, were grown for medicinal reasons because it was thought to be an amazing cure-all, hence the common name. Today, the petals are candied or crystallized for confectionery or bakery and made into oils, ointments, waters, and simple or concentrated acid infusions for pharmaceutical purposes.

❑ Lime-blossom tea is both soothing and refreshing. Fruit teas are easily prepared by infusion with boiling water.

The flowers of *Calendula officinalis* come in shades of cream, lemon and apricot, but for culinary colour there is no substitute for orange.

The flowers, leaves and seeds of the annual nasturtium, *Tropaeolum majus*, make a tasty addition to salads. The leaves and seeds add a spicy quality to the dish.

Borage is rich in potassium salts - the juice contains 30 percent nitrate of potash. Borage leaves are said to make a reviving sandwich filler.

Marigold flowers can be used fresh or dried. Grow them in an area away from pollution and chemical sprays.

Medicinal flowers

Any plant that has '*officinalis*' as part of its name means that it has been used for centuries as a herb of healing. *Melilotus officinalis*, for example, is a tall, rather weedy-looking biennial found in Europe and eastwards to China. Its pale yellow flowers provide abundant pollen and nectar for insect visitors, but for all its delicate appearance, this is a powerful plant containing vitamin C, and is used as an antispasmodic, a diuretic, a sedative and for healing wounds. The dried flowers are used as an infusion or syrup to treat catarrh and thrombosis and externally for inflammation and suppurating wounds. A distillation is said to alleviate conjunctivitis. Chamomile, *Chamaemelum nobile*, is a low, much-branched herb from Europe, North Africa and the Azores, that grows to about 40cm(16in), with dissected, apple-scented leaves and white daisylike flowers with yellow centres. It is cultivated as a herbal medicine; the dried flowers are a sedative and have an anti-inflammatory effect, acting as a mild disinfectant. They are made into infusions, an essence, a tincture, a fluid extract, a syrup and a powder to treat diarrhoea, skin eruptions, ulcers, and to reduce fever and promote appetite. A rubbing oil is also manufactured for applying to painful joints and swellings.

A distillation of the dried flowers of the ox-eye daisy alleviates coughs and asthma. Poultices of the fresh plant may be applied to slow-healing wounds.

This medicinal rose produces only one set of flowers each year. At the height of its popularity, when vast quantities of the blooms were needed, huge fields of it were kept under cultivation.

Melilot flowers have been used in herbal medicine for centuries. They contain Vitamin C and can be used either fresh or dried for a wide range of medical purposes, from reducing inflammation to promoting restful sleep.

❏ The large, ragged, orange-yellow daisies of *Arnica montana* are used as a tincture, infusion, fluid extract and salve for the external treatment of bruises, wounds, lumbago and sciatica.

❏ The pale mauve flowers of rosemary, *Rosmarinus officinalis*, can be boiled down into a substance to combat wrinkles, while a distillation of the fragrant flowers of lily-of-the-valley, *Convallaria majalis*, acts as a facial astringent.

❏ Sloe-blossom, *Prunus spinosa*, makes a gentle laxative and an infusion of the pink flowers of annual centaury, *Centaurium erythraea*, relieves indigestion.

❏ The dried leaves and flowers of feverfew, *Tanacetum parthenium,* prepared as a tea are good for migraine. Wild mignonette, *Reseda lutea*, has spikes of sweet-scented greenish flowers which can be dried and used to stuff pillows to mitigate insomnia and induce sleep. An infusion of the flowers alleviates asthma and hay-fever, and can be used externally to treat wounds and soothe inflamed eyes.

❏ The dried flowers of meadowsweet, *Filipendula ulmaria,* can be made into an infusion said to be effective in the treatment of influenza, rheumatism, fevers, blood disorders, diabetes, dysentery, diarrhoea and colic.

At one time, the apothecary's rose, *Rosa officinalis*, was a common cure-all. Today, the petals are only used in infusions, to make rose-oil, rose-water, ointment, eyedrops and an astringent.

The flowers of golden-rod, *Solidago virgaurea*, are used in infusions, a tincture, a fluid extract and a syrup to treat digestive disorders, kidney complaints, coughs, skin conditions, thrush and internal bleeding. They provide a late-summer feast for bees, and in the wild would ensure the survival of the hive through winter.

Economically important flowers

Certain flowers have acquired an astonishing commercial value. For example, it takes about 60,000 stigmas of the saffron crocus, *Crocus sativus*, to make 450gm(16oz) of saffron. Expensive stuff, as the dangling orange-red stigmas are the only part of the flower used. This crocus has been cultivated in Mediterranean countries since the time of Solomon, and was an important trade commodity even then. In eastern Asia, saffron-yellow was considered a royal colour and also has religious significance. For centuries it was used as a dye, in perfumery and cosmetics, in medicine and as a flavouring. It is still used today, although synthetic substitutes are becoming more commonplace. Flowers that are commercially important for their fragrance are many and varied. A classic example is lavender, *Lavandula officinalis*. Vast fields of this Mediterranean plant are cultivated for the perfumery trade, and the extracted oil is also used in herbal medicine, as an antiseptic and an insecticide. For drying, the flowers are picked before they are fully open on sunny days, but cutting for oil extraction is carried out in the cooler mornings and evenings, when there is no hot sun to dissipate the aromatic compounds. From June onwards, the fragrant, organic oils are found in all the green parts of the plant, but after June they become concentrated in the flower spikes and can be seen as minute glistening globules. The flowers build up their maximum fragrance in July, when the flowers are fully expanded and fill the air with their heady perfume. Rose-growing is internationally important, both for the sale of the plants and for the perfume industry. The Romans used roses in their ceremonials and imported them from Egypt, where they flowered earlier than in the cooler northern Mediterranean, until their own plants came into bloom.

The saffron crocus, *Crocus sativus*, showing the orange-red stigmas from which saffron is made. Do not confuse this member of the iris family with the autumn crocus, *Colchicum autumnale*, a poisonous species.

These roses are grown commercially in Khotan in China, where thousands of blooms are harvested by hand and made into rose wine.

❏ The dried and powdered flowers of pyrethrum (shown above), *Chrysanthemum cinerariifolium*, are used to make a non-toxic insecticide.

❏ Hops, *Humulus lupulus*, are lusty twining plants that grow vigorously in summer. The delicate, pale green hops are pendent, cone-shaped clusters of bracts enclosing the small female flowers - the male flowers are not commercially used. Yellow resin glands at the base of the bracts produce drops of 'lupulin', which gives beer its distinctive flavour.

❏ Cloves are the dried flower-buds of the tropical tree, *Eugenia caryophyllus*.

These are the female flowers of the hop plant, grown commercially to flavour beer, and also for herbal medicines. The green, star-shaped male flowers occur on separate plants and are not harvested.

All lavenders smell powerfully similar, but this one, *Lavandula officinalis*, is the most widely grown commercially. The extracted oil is used in herbal medicine, as an insecticide and for perfume.

Flowers as artistic inspiration

Long before man could write, he began to carve and paint, and centuries later we are still admiring the vitality of his cave drawings. Flowers have always been an inspiration to artists and designers. The Egyptians created formalized and even naturalistic paintings of everything around them and among their most frequent subjects were the lotus flower and the papyrus, which appear in architecture, on tomb-furniture, decorated tomb-ceilings, mummy-cases and jewellery. Chinese and Japanese flower artists revered their subject and adopted a humble approach to their painting. They sought to retain the 'habit' of the flower, even though for the purposes of the work, the subject may have been modified. To the botanically minded, this artistic licence may have been carried too far at times. In the eleventh century, during the Sung dynasty, the Chinese painter Kuo Hsi advised his pupils always to observe the plant carefully before beginning to paint. This is just as valid now, 900 years later. Early Moslem artists avoided naturalistic representation and preferred stylization or abstraction; nevertheless, plant forms such as palms, the lotus and the chrysanthemum constantly appear, often combined with the traditional swirling arabesque. The sacred lotus, *Nelumbo nucifera*, occurs in recognizable form in the art of all the ancient civilizations of the Near, Middle and Far East. It was the symbol of purity, because it rose, unsullied and beautiful, from the mud and slime of the lake bed. Buddah is invariably portrayed seated on a lotus flower, in which it is said he was born. In the 15th and 16th centuries, flowers were regularly portrayed with loving skill in prayer books, religious texts and a wide range of beautifully prepared illuminated manuscripts.

The Persians used many flowers in their designs, in naturalistic and stylized forms, including the iris, lily, dianthus and rose, all featured in this eighteenth-century Persian prayer rug. Their best work dates from the Safavid period, from 1502 to 1736.

The Chinese used sumptuously petalled peonies and chrysanthemums in paintings, embroideries, wall hangings and on porcelain. Plum blossom was revered because it symbolized rebirth and the end of winter. This dish was produced between 1661 and 1722.

This picture, taken at Karnak in Egypt, shows stylized papyrus plants on a column in the temple of Amun. The papyrus was a symbol of lower Egypt and appeared in all stages of growth on Egyptian architecture, tomb-furniture, decorated ceilings, as well as sarcophagi and jewellery.

An artist paints tree peonies, a flower much associated with centuries of Chinese art and design. It has appeared on porcelain, carpets, fabrics, paper, metalwork and papier-mache.

❏ The Greeks used stylized but recognizable images of honeysuckle, laurel, ivy and, of course, the vine, as inspiration for many of their designs.

❏ There is a formalized painting of Madonna lilies (shown above) on a wall in Amnisos, near Knossos on the island of Crete, which was completed in about 1550 B.C. Much later, this lily became a Christian symbol of purity and is depicted in religious paintings. Also at Knossos, a painting from about 2000 B.C. shows a roselike flower, its earliest identifiable depiction.

❏ The conception of formalized 'rose' windows, such as those at Chartres, Laon and Notre Dame, began in the twelfth century with plate tracery, in which patterns were formed by perforating large expanses of flat stone.

Endangered and disappearing species

Today, there is an increasing awareness of the importance of protecting and preserving the many irreplaceable species of plants and animals under threat in the modern world. Currently, about 25,000 species of plant are in imminent danger of extinction. In the rainforests of South America, for example, plant and animal species of all kinds are vanishing before they can be properly classified. Increasing urbanization, modern farming methods and pollution, as well as natural predators, have taken their toll of the habitats of many wild plants worldwide. Their very rarity makes certain plants desirable 'collector's items'. One such is the UK species of the lady's slipper orchid, *Cypripedium calceolus*, which is placed under day-and-night watch when it is due to flower at its one remaining site in England. The lady's slipper is large for a temperate orchid, with a maroon perianth and a pouched yellow lip, or labellum. It takes about 15 years for the plant to come to its first flowering from seed. Similarly under threat – from both collectors and insect infestation – is the silversword, *Argyroxiphium sandwicense*, from Hawaii and Maui. Also endangered is the giant forget-me-not, *Myosotidium hortensia*, of the Chatham Islands in the Pacific Ocean off the east coast of South Island, New Zealand. The habitat of this handsome plant, with its corymbs of sky-blue flowers, has been altered by grazing animals and it now survives only in inaccessible rocky niches by the seashore. Although it is difficult to grow, its survival, like that of the silversword and many other plants, may ultimately depend on the sanctuaries provided by botanical gardens, national parks and dedicated gardeners.

The very rare Chatham Island forget-me-not is said to enjoy a mulch of seaweed when grown away from its native habitat in the South Pacific. Here it survives in rocky crevices, away from browsing animals.

The cowslip, *Primula veris*, was once a feature of the chalk downlands of England. The destruction of its habitat means that this orange-scented flower that Shakespeare knew is becoming very scarce.

The lady's slipper orchid is very rare in England. The remaining plants are protected when it flowers in early summer. This is the American species, similar in appearance and pollinating mechanism.

The haleakala silversword of Maui in Hawaii is endangered owing to its collectability in past years, and to the recent infestation of several insect pests that feed on the flowers. These very striking plants take 20 years to bloom.

❏ The curious closed flowers of the devil's claw, *Phyteuma comosum*, are found only on certain Austrian mountains, where the plant is protected, and on mountain sites in Italy, where it is not. The style grows out through the closed petals, pushing pollen ahead of it.

❏ *Hibiscus insularis* is almost extinct in its wild habitat on Philip Island in the Pacific Ocean. Once lush, the island has been grazed by goats, pigs and rabbits, and the soil has eroded into the sea.

❏ The handsome *Protea grandiceps* (above) is already extinct in some of its South African habitats, although it can still be found in a few locations. There are several reasons for this. Firstly, it has been over-enthusiastically 'collected'. Secondly, local bush-fires have destroyed many plants, and lastly, only a few viable seeds are produced from each flower and these do not appear until this slow-growing bush is mature. Fortunately, it is cultivated for its beauty by gardeners.

SUPERFACTS

SUPERFACTS

The earliest flowers ▲

Simple, magnolia-like blooms are known to have been among the first flowers to develop in the Cretaceous period, up to 136 million years ago. Their organs of reproduction evolved from a spiral shape into a circle and have changed little since. The magnolia above shows a pinkish petal at the lefthand edge that is intermediate in shape and colour between the crimson stamens and the white petals - an interesting 'halfway house'.

Vegetable flower buds

Early man was at first nomadic but eventually became a farmer by the end of the Stone Age, settling down to grow what suited the surroundings and his immediate needs. By the early 19th century, he had learned to accelerate the process of selection, and the results are the food plants that we know today, such as huge cauliflowers and even larger cabbages. These vegetables are actually enlarged flower buds, where the generative organs have been transformed or bred out.

Ancient survivor ▼

Welwitschia mirabilis, shown below, is a unique plant, similar to no other in the whole plant kingdom. It looks something like a giant, closed-in, wooden egg-cup, with a huge water-storing root, enabling it to survive the almost waterless conditions of its remote desert habitat in Nambia (South West Africa). It is surrounded by what seems to be a tangle of leathery leaves, actually only two, whose split and shredded appearance is due to the constant erosion of the elements, although the leaves continue to grow from the base throughout the plant's long life, which can be over a hundred years. *Welwitschia* produces stalks of male or female cones from the rim of the crown on separate male and female plants. The female ovules are borne naked, showing this plant to be a primitive gymnosperm.

Sun-seeking Adonis

The yellow adonis, *Adonis vernalis,* a member of the buttercup family, Ranunculaceae, has no nectar, but provides plenty of pollen for its many insect visitors, such as bees, butterflies, flies and beetles. It is a true flower of the sun, opening out quite flat, but only in bright sunlight. If a prolonged spell of bad weather prevents insects from visiting, the flower can adopt another strategy and pollinate itself later in the season. The seed of another buttercup, *Ranunculus acris*, was found buried under a Roman fort in Cumberland in the UK, dating from about AD 117.

Short-lived flowers ▲

The delicate flowers of *Cyanotis speciosum* are very short-lived, lasting but a few hours in the searing desert heat of the Yemen day. It is related to that well-known houseplant called spiderwort or tradescantia.

Another short-lived flower that must attract its insect pollinators quickly is *Capparis spinosa*, the Hawaiian Puapilo. This straggling shrub produces scented white flowers that open only at night; these then fade to pink when pollinated and wither at sunrise. The flowers have long tubes suited to moth pollinators and are in bloom all year round, although more productive of blossom after the autumn rains. The pickled flowerbuds are the capers used for cooking and flavouring.

The flowers of the succulent *Anacampseros* are truly ephemeral, lasting only for an hour or so. In the desert, the plant must conserve its precious water resources and moisture is lost when the petals are open. The flowers are self-pollinating.

Timing is everything

When different species of flowers bloom in the same place at the same time, they are competing for the attentions of a wide range of insect pollinators. This has led to the many differences in flower colour, size, shape and scent. To attract pollinators, flowers may open at different times of the day, with nectar and pollen at peak quality, or they may bloom sequentially during the year, thus maintaining a supply of food for the pollinators, which must form colonies and breed. If, say, a bumblebee ceases to visit specific or 'sympathetic' flowers, to which each is adapted, then the nectar level will rise and become accessible to other and shorter-tongued insects.

Natural variety

Mutations occur constantly among wild plants - it is part of the ongoing process of evolution. In the wild, such mutations are the result of the coincidental and fortuitous actions of heat, cold, the environment and the naturally occurring radiations that combine to produce modifications within the plant's cells. A mutation is an immediate change in a gene or chromosome, showing itself in the plant as a permanent change in an inheritable character. The plants carrying the new characteristics hybridize with each other (within the species) resulting in new varieties. Many are eliminated by outside circumstances, such as competition, but others will flourish, succeeding where the parents could not. Flower breeders have simply focused and directed this natural tendency for change.

The largest flowering family

The Compositae family, with a worldwide distribution, consists of no less than 900 genera and more than 13,000 species. Many familiar flowers belong to it, including asters, sunflowers chrysanthemums and zinnias.

The world's largest flower ▼

Rafflesia arnoldii has no green coloration whatsoever. It is a total parasite, taking its nourishment from the exposed roots of specific tropical vines. In due season it produces a woody-looking bud that quickly expands into the huge, foul-smelling exotic-looking flower shown below, often measuring 90cm(36in) across. Finding an example is cause for celebration; *Rafflesia* is becoming increasingly rare owing to the destruction of its jungle habitat.

Colour-matched flowers

The tall delphiniums and the closely related larkspurs are mainly blue in the UK, where the pollinators are usually bees, which cannot see red. In the USA, where hummingbirds act as pollinators, the delphinium is red, as are some types of columbines (*Aquilegia*), whose flowers are rewardingly rich in nectar.

Chemical colour change

Some flowers, such as the mop-head *Hydrangea macrophylla*, have been developed by plant-breeders into complete sterility and are propagated vegetatively. Even colours can be changed artificially, pink flowers being induced to flower blue by the application of aluminium sulphate. Blue-flowering hydrangeas normally occur on acid soil, but as large, long-lasting blue flowers are very attractive in the garden, many gardeners 'improve' on nature. On alkaline soil, blue varieties turn pink or crimson. On acid soils, the blooms of pink varieties turn mauve, but annual dressings of ground limestone to the soil restore the normal pink coloration.

SUPERFACTS

Ingenious insect traps

Flowers have evolved ingenious ways of trapping insects. *Ceropegia rendalli* (shown below) from the Transvaal has small, 2.5cm(1in) tubular flowers with frilled green lobes. The interior of the fluted funnel has downward-pointing hairs covered in a slippery oil that allows small insect visitors to crawl past to the nectar. Once inside, they cannot get out. Escape is impossible until the pollen is liberated and the flower tube wilts. *Ceropegia* relies for pollination on these small flies, which transfer sticky pollen masses on their legs, and lures them with a scent that is powerful to the flies but faint to the human nose. Other types of *Ceropegia* are called 'lantern flowers' and these attract female flies and midges only by reproducing the reassuring smell of the egg-laying phase of the female insects' sexual cycle. One such is *Ceropegia grandis,* which has translucent 'windows' in the complex flowers that prevent the inside of the flower from being too dark - most pollinating insects avoid darkness.

Buzz pollination

The ripe anthers of most flowers release pollen by splitting open lengthways and the pollen grains then either fall out or are scooped out by visiting insects. But certain flowers have anthers with only a small opening at one end. Pollen-collecting bees clasp the anthers tightly and vibrate their bodies, shaking the anthers so that the pollen falls out onto the bees' hairy abdomen, later to be transferred to the next flower. During this exercise, the bees make a short, sharp buzzing noise that can be heard quite a distance away. The vibration is caused by contracting the flight muscles, which in turn sets the thoracic skeleton and its clasping legs into oscillation. The bees' wings hardly move during the operation. Honeybees do not do this. Among flowers with this type of anther are the nightshade family and rhododendron. They produce no nectar and very small pollen grains with little pollen-glue, so the grains can be 'buzz-shaken' out evenly when ripe.

Conserving vital water

Desert plants have developed many methods of conserving water. Some are succulent, with thick leaves and stems. They store moisture in their aerial parts and are plump and firm after rain, gradually shrinking as the water is used up. Others have a reduced or non-existent leaf-surface area between rains. Many have wide or very deep-rooting systems, some reaching down as much as 20m(66ft). Many desert plants produce their flowers at night when they lose less water than in the heat of day.

The passion flower legend

The legend dates back to the 16th century, when the Jesuits followed the victorious Conquistadores to South America. Needing a good omen for the future, the Jesuits found one as they stepped ashore: a trailing, woody, climbing plant - most probably *Passiflora coerulea* - which they named the passion flower. To them, the ten sepals and petals (five of each, similarly coloured) represented the ten loyal apostles - Judas and doubting Thomas being left out - and the 'corona' of threadlike growths symbolized the crown of thorns. The five stamens were the five wounds of Christ, the three-part stigma symbolized the three nails and the ovary was the hammer that drove them in. The spiralling, curling tendrils were the scourging whips, and the palmate leaves represented the grasping hands of the soldiers. Soon after, the Jesuits found the native Indians eating the yellow fruits and interpreted this as a desire for Christianity. The plant has extra-floral nectaries at the base of the leaf-stalks to divert non-pollinating visitors from the true floral nectaries.

Automatic pollen dispenser

The brown-rayed knapweed - *Centaurea jacea* - is a good example of a 'head' flower. It has many small tubular flowers grouped tightly together on the outside edge; these are sterile and mainly for show. The fertile inner florets have pollen threads that shorten by about a third in a few seconds when touched by an insect. The closed anther tube is pulled downward and the style within acts like a piston to push the pollen up towards the insect. After all the pollen has been collected, the style grows out of the anther tube, ready to accept pollen from another flower.

The largest inflorescence

A wisteria vine in California is claimed to have branches 152m(500ft) long and to produce 1.5 million blossoms during its five-week flowering period.

Scent collectors

Some tropical bees are known as 'orchid bees'. They have brilliant metallic coloration and enlarged tibias on their hind legs that have developed into containers for flower-scents. The six bees shown below may all be collecting scent, in which case all are males, since females have no such storage capacity. It is not known yet why bees do this, but during the process of collection the flowers are pollinated.

Drunk on nectar

Butterflies can sometimes become intoxicated on nectar when they sip from matured *Buddleia*, *Inula* or other flowers, and the same fate appears to have befallen the bees shown below. They appear to be trapped within these *Dendrobium* orchid flowers, but *Dendrobium* has no 'trapping' mechanism, such as is found in the cruel plant, *Araujia sericofera*. In the Northern Hemisphere, exhausted bees sometimes stay overnight in suitable flowers, such as the big, purple, thistle-like blooms of the globe artichoke. If the night is cool, they must wait for the sun's rays to warm them sufficiently before they can fly away.

Natural energy drink

Nectar is basically a watery solution of sugars - glucose, fructose and sucrose - with the sugar content amounting to about 40 percent, although this varies quite widely according to the plant species. Other substances present in nectar include proteins, amino-acids, phosphates, organic acids, enzymes and vitamins. The quality of the nectar can vary quite considerably throughout a 24-hour period. Nectar is often made available by the plant on a daily basis; when conditions are right, a single flower can produce from one to five milligrams of nectar each day. According to the type of plant, the sugar content can vary appreciably, although the amount available may be constant. In other flowers, the quality is unvarying but the flow is not. Generally speaking, the nectar is at its best when the sun is shining on the flower, with the day-temperature increasing and the humidity lessening. Bees are capable of learning the point in the day when the quality of the nectar in the flowers they are visiting will be at its best. Then they take their fill of this natural and sustaining energy drink.

Pollinating strategies

Some flowers, such as the yellow mountain saxifrage, *Saxifraga aizoides*, use various strategies to avoid self-pollination. All their anthers fall off after the pollen has gone, leaving the female parts to continue with their development. Quantities of nectar are produced to attract pollinating flies and later, when any potency of the plant's own pollen is too aged to be effective, the stigmas develop, ready to receive pollen from other, different flowers. The opposite is the case with the semi-tropical climber *Cobaea scandens*, which is usually pollinated by bats. If no bat visits the short-lived flowers, the stamens eventually move so that self-pollination takes place just before the flower wilts and falls to the ground. The monkey flower, *Mimulus*, has a device that operates as soon as the stigma is touched by an insect. The lobes close up, gripping compatible pollen tightly so that it can begin its journey down the pollen-tubes, but relax if the pollen is unsuitable.

Suddenly scentless

Mimulus (or musk) was once very highly scented and cherished as a pot-plant because of this. Then, almost simultaneously, all the plants all over the world lost their scent and no satisfactory explanation has been given. Today, the flowers are scentless.

Flowers among gods

In Indian art, Buddha is often portrayed seated on a stylized lotus flower, or carrying one of the flowers in his hand. This is the pink sacred lotus, *Nelumbo nucifera*. Another Indian deity, the feminine Tara, appears as a beautiful girl holding a long-stemmed lotus that represents transcendent wisdom, the goal of Buddhist study. Some divine figures occur with a palm-leaf book supported on a lotus. It is known that the seeds of the American lotus, *Nelumbo lutea*, popularly known as 'water chinkapin', retain their ability to germinate for about 1,000 years.

SUPERFACTS

Room for all

Nature has developed many ways of sharing out its rewards. In the USA, goldenrod (*Solidago*) is a prolifically flowering late-summer bee plant, and all kinds of bees can be seen feeding on it. The bees do not waste their precious energy in confronting other bees; instead, the smaller species simply retreat to the outer ends of the flower sprays that are too weak to support the greater weight of the large bumblebees, which feed nearer to the centre of the plant. Individual goldenrod flowers do not contain much nectar, but each plant may produce over 1,000 yellow blossoms.

Slow-growing cycad

A specimen of the Mexican cycad, *Dioon edule*, was found to have grown to only 2m(78in) in 1,000 years. Each year, the plant adds a few fronds to its crown to replace the old ones, which slowly fragment, leaving a scar on the trunk. It is possible to estimate the age of the tree by counting these scars and the number of new leaves added to the crown.

Pollen overload

Many flowers produce excessive quantities of pollen, far more than seems necessary. Heather is one example, manufacturing vast amounts of fine, light pollen in addition to nectar, which bees make into honey. It seems that this plant, like others, is capable of wind and insect pollination. The red field poppy, *Papaver rhoeas*, is another plant that produces even more pollen than many wind-pollinated flowers.

King of the cacti

The slow-growing *Saguaro* cactus (above) is the largest of all cacti and is protected by law. This does not stop 'cactus-rustlers' from driving out into the desert at night, where they use winches to haul the huge plants out of the ground in order to sell them to collectors. The great root system which supports the cactus is cut, and the shock to the mature plants is generally too much for them and inevitably they die. Seedlings are becoming scarcer all the time because of the changes in the now-fragile desert ecology. Left to themselves, cacti can survive almost anything but times have changed. The settlers introduced cattle into the deserts of Mexico and the southwestern areas of the United States. The cattle ate such grass as there was, and this had hitherto concealed and protected the tender saguaro seedlings from wood-rats. The open spaces became colonized by other more vigorously growing cacti that harboured more wood-rats, which in turn ate all the green vegetation indiscriminately, including the emerging saguaro seedlings. Full-grown *Saguaros* are very tall and because of their height are often struck by lightning during the sudden and violent desert storms. A direct strike will usually kill or damage them beyond recovery.

Undercover beauties

Two members of the orchid family live totally underground lives. *Rhizanthella slateri* and the closely related and very similar *Rhizanthella gardneri* are saprophytes and were discovered accidentally. They have no green coloration whatever. *Rhizanthella slateri* produces and matures its waxy white flowers some 2cm(0.8in) below the soil surface. The flowers are less than 0.6cm(0.25in) across, and 15 to 30 of them are crowded together. When exposed to light, the flowers change to a purplish colour. It is not yet known how they are pollinated, but ripe ovaries contain fertile seeds and, after fertilization, the seedpods elongate until they are just level with the soil surface. It is thought that this ensures seed distribution. These strange orchids are found in separate areas of western Australia.

Dizzy heights

The common sunflower can grow to amazing heights. One garden specimen grew to 6.54m(over 21ft) tall.

Absorbing leaves

The leaves of tamarisk secrete a solution of calcium chloride that attracts moisture, which is in turn absorbed by the leaf system, enabling the shrub to survive in apparently waterless conditions. It also puts down deep roots.

Three-in-one flowers

Featured below is an extreme example of the result of combined plant breeding and bonsai culture. Three different varieties of *Prunus persica* are flowering together on one stem.

The man orchid ▶

The man orchid (*Aceras anthropophorum*), shown right looks exactly like a small, hooded human figure, and because of this and the shape of the tubers, which resemble testicles, this 'man-plant' was used in early magic to excite or restrain desire, although never as much as the more universal early purple orchid, *Orchis mascula*. (The Greek word for testicle is *orchis*.) There can be as many as 90 flowers on a well-grown plant, all with nectar, making them very attractive to flies and hover-flies.

Pretty but ruthless

The European butterworts (*Pinguicula*) are pretty but ruthless, often killing their insect visitors by one means or another. *Pinguicula alpina* is a deadly little plant, growing in marshy places that abound in the small flies that act as pollinators. The entrance to the white flower has two little bumps or mounds covered in yellow hairs that are attractive to flies, which alight and crawl into the spur at the back of the plant, which in other plants often contains nectar. But the butterwort's spur is empty of sweetness, although there is food of another kind. The flies gorge themselves and then try to crawl out backwards, but are prevented by a thick growth of inward-pointing hairs on which they have just been resting. A strong and clever fly will take its time and extricate itself gradually, pushing upwards with its body to free itself from the hairs. The upward movement causes its back to be brushed with pollen. Weak flies remain clasped by the hairs and die there. The butterwort also traps other, smaller flies in the gummy secretion exuded by its

leaves, after which it produces another fluid that digests them. The flowers are protogynous (starting as female and becoming male). A successful fly pollinates the flowers by transporting pollen from older male flowers to young female ones.

Attractive and insatiable

Water hyacinth has been called the 'rabbit of the plant world'. Calculations have shown that if left unchecked the progeny from one plant could cover all the freshwater areas in the world within two years, providing that sufficient nourishment were available. The rootless water hyacinth blocks any constricted waterway in which it grows, fouling ship's propellers and water-pumps. But recent research has shown that the plant can clear the water in which it floats of poisonous pollutants.

Myths and superstitions

As well as being one of the world's best 'bee' flowers, clover was formerly regarded as a lucky plant, bringing nothing but good and sometimes bestowing the gift of 'second sight'.

Heavily scented flowers are very disturbing to some people. Once they were called 'drowsy scented' and people believed that it was unlucky to sleep in the same room with them lest the sleeper never awoke. They were also believed to shelter the souls of the dead.

Actors refuse to have real flowers on stage because they are believed to bring bad luck. End-of-performance bouquets are not included in this belief because they are not part of the production.

Red flowers of any kind are thought to bring good luck, because red is the colour of blood and therefore of life and love. Red roses in particular are symbolic of success in love.

In some parts of the world it is regarded as bad luck to take mixed red and white flowers to a sick person or into a hospital. They are thought to pressage a death, but not necessarily of the recipient.

Marigolds once symbolized constancy and endurance in love, and were used in old-time wedding garlands and love charms. In Eastern Europe, a spell to ensure a lover's constancy was to secretly dig earth from his footprints, put it into a pot and sow marigold

seeds into it. Dreaming of the flowers in bloom signified wealth to come. The flower heads applied to bee or wasp stings were said to soothe the pain. And if a man looked long and deeply into marigold flowers, he would be safe from 'fevers, agues and pestilence' on that day.

Orange blossom has strong wedding connotations, superseding the far older belief in the flowers of rosemary and myrtle. The orange tree symbolizes fertility, and a sprig of blossom in a bride's bouquet or headdress meant that she would bear children. The golden fruits were once used in many different love charms.

One step from extinction ▼

Knowlton's cactus, below, is said to be the rarest cactus in the world. This photograph shows only too clearly how easy it is to destroy these small and fragile plants.

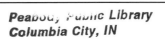

103

INDEX

Page numbers in **bold** indicate major references, including accompanying photographs. Page numbers in *italics* indicate captions to illustrations. Other entries are in normal type.

The paired tubular flowers of this trumpet honeysuckle, *Lonicera sempervirens*, are irresistible to insect pollinators.

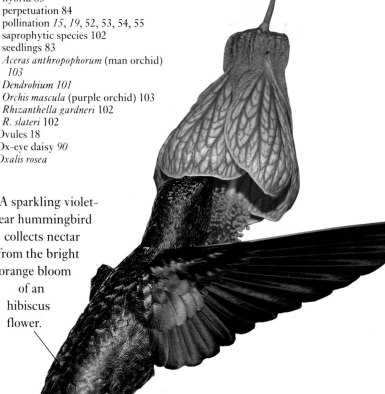

A sparkling violet-ear hummingbird collects nectar from the bright orange bloom of an hibiscus flower.

Index compiled by Stuart Craik.

PICTURE CREDITS

The publishers wish to thank the following photographers and
agencies who have supplied photographs for this book. The
photographers have been credited by page number and position on
the page: (B)Bottom, (T)Top, (C)Centre, (BL)Bottom Left, etc.

C. Bakelaar: 99(T), 100(BL)

Biofotos:
Heather Angel: 6, 16-17(C), 17(BR), 33(BR),
35(B), 43(BR), 45(T), 50-1(T), 53(R), 54(TR),
62-3(TC), 64(TL), 71(TL), 80(B), 82(B),
84(BL), 87(TR), 93(BL,R), 95(B), 96(BL),
103(T)
Brian Rogers: 34(B)

Dr J.C. Chubb: 100(T)

Eric Crichton: Title page, 10(BR), 11(BR), 14-
15(C), 29(TC), 47(CR), 49(CB), 65(B), 67(T),
74(BL), 75(C), 81(B,R), 83(TR), 87(TR,TL),
89(T)

C.M. Dixon: 94-5(T), 94(BL), 95(T,R),
101(T)

Ron & Christine Foord: Front endpaper,
30(B), 30-1(TC), 31(CR), 38-9(TC,BC),
49(BR), 50, 55(TL), 57(CR), 63(CR), 85(T,R)

G.S.F. Picture Library: 63(TR, Dr. F. Taylor)

Di Lewis: 88(BL)

Natural Science Photos:

P.A. Bowman: 53(TL), 55(R)
Jeremy Burgess: 31(C)
W. Cane: 18(BL,BR), 19(T), 97(T)
M. Chinery: 12-13(CT), 58-9(CR), 78(BL)
Stephen Davis: 64-5(CB)
Martin and Dorothy Grace: 90-1(C)
M. Harvey: 98(B)
D. Meredith: 57(T)
T.A. Moss: 26(BL), 27(TR)
Richard Revels: 54(BL), 66(BL), 83(TL)
P.H. Ward: 35(T), 83(B)
P.H. Ward & S.L. Ward: 51(BL)

Don Watt: 20(TL)
Curtis E. Williams: 24-5(T), 41(TR)
D. Yendall: 56-7(CB), 76(BL)

Maurice Nimmo: 10(BL), 43(TR), 46-7(C),
70, 71(TR), 88-9(C), 89(R)

Frans Noltee: 42-3(CB)

Oxford Scientific Films: 75(R, Sean Morris)

Photo Researchers Inc.:
Mark N. Boulton: 32(B), 74-5(B)
John Bova: 60(BL)
Ken Brate: 26-7(TC)
Richard Weymouth Brooks: 102(T)
Scott Camazine: 12(B), 35(CR), 52(B)
Patricia Caulfield: 39(BR)
Ray Coleman: 13(C)
Stephen E. Cornelius: 59(R)
Stephen Dalton: 22-3(B)
R. Dev: 72-3(C)
Joe DiStefano: 11(TL), 15(TC)
Ray Ellis: Back endpaper
R.J. Erwin: 44-5(TC)
Ray Fairbanks: 37(TL)
Kenneth W. Fink: 45(TR)
Gilbert Grant: 28-9(C)
Farrell Grehan: 68-9(B), 85(B)
Francois Gohier: 72
Don Guravich: 87(R)
Robert W. Hernandez: 66-7(B)
John Kaprielian: 20(BL)
Krafft-Explorer: 62(BL)
Steven J. Krasemann: 5, 65(T,CR), 79(T),
103(BR)
Frans Lanting: 24(BL)
Calvin Larsen: 46(BL)
Angelina Lax: 80-1(T)
Pat & Tom Leeson: 77(TR)
Jeff Lepore: 14(BL), 105
Craig K. Lorenz: 78(T)

Michael Lustbader: 71(BR), 73(TR)
Emil Muench: 92
Tom McHugh: 93(BR)
Pertti Nikkila: 73(B)
Stephen P. Parker: 60(BC)
Daniele Pellegrini: 56(TL)
Rod Planck: 86, 96-7(C)
Porterfield-Chickering: 33(TR)
Andrew Rakoczy: 41
Bonnie Rauch: 8
H. Reinhard/Okapia: 62-3(B)
L.W. Richardson: 77(R)
J.H. Robinson: 26-7(BR)
R. Rowan: 97(BR)
Kjell B. Sandved: 29(TR,BR), 36, 52(C),
69(T), 101(B)
Jany Sauvanet: 25(BR)
Jerry Schad: 76-7(B)
Gregory K. Scott: 40(BL), 49(TR)
Dan Suzio: 29(BL), 40-1(TC), 58-9(CL)
Anton Thielemann/Okapia: 21
Norm Thomas: 78-9(B)
Merlin D. Tuttle: 23(TC,TR)
M.W.F. Tweedie: 21(TR), 99(B)
Karl Weidmann: 106
L. West: 47(T)
Jerome Wexler: 19(BR), 48-9(T)
Dr. Paul A. Zahl: 69(CR)

G.R. Roberts: 16(BL), 17(CR), 22-3(TC),
32-3(TC), 38(BL), 44(BL), 60-1(C), 76-7(T),
89(BR), 98(T)

Daan Smit: 15(R), 24-5(BC), 37(B,TR),
42-3(TC), 43(TC), 45(B), 48(BL), 51(BR),
57(B), 58(BL), 69(BR), 71(BL), 82(TL), 84-
5(C), 90(BL), 91(T), 93(T), 97(R), 102(B)

Wildlife Matters (Dr John Feltwell): 66(TR),
91(B)

108